Dancing On Stones:
A Quest for Joy

by
Edith Harrington

————◆————

Dancing On Stones:
A Quest for Joy

by
Edith Harrington

————◆————

Gannah's Gate

Dancing on Stones: A Quest for Joy

ISBN-13: 978-1-946985-05-7

All the events related in this book are true as
described. However, some minor details, including
names of individuals, have been changed to maintain
anonymity.

Edited by Yvonne Anderson
Cover photo of Maria Khoreva used by permission

Cover design by Eye-Catcher Book Covers
eyecatcherbookcovers@outlook.com

∞

Acknowledgements

∞

To the King of Kings and Lord of Lords I give all honour and praise, for it is He who set me on this journey, walked beside me the entire way, and prompted me to write the story.

God used many human instruments in this process, but I would like to thank in particular two gifted women whom He brought into my life through a series of "coincidences."

The first is Ellen Tarver. After reading my first draft, she encouraged me to keep going. Thank you, Ellen, for your insightful suggestions and support.

The second is Yvonne Anderson. Thank you, Yvonne, for sharing your literary expertise to hone and shape my manuscript into the book it is today.

Finally, I thank Maria Khoreva for allowing me to use her photo on the cover.

Table of Contents

‿‿
Introduction
‿‿

Pray through to victory! Name it and claim it by faith, and it is yours! These were the catch cries of my church.

I named and claimed, fasted and prayed…but nothing changed.

Why was I suffering? Why were my prayers unanswered? What was wrong with me?

Trying to reconcile my life with what my church taught drove me to the edge of mental breakdown.

This is my story.

∽

Chapter 1

∽

Dance

A YOUNG COUPLE moved through the bustle of the after-church crush. Hand in hand, they stood beaming at my husband and me, each waiting for the other to speak first.

Finally, the young man stammered, "We're being married, as you know. And, well, we were wondering if you two would dance during the signing of the register?" The young woman nodded enthusiastically.

Alistair asked, "Do you have a piece of music in mind?"

The young woman tipped her head. "Well, no, not exactly. But we really like that harp and flute piece you danced to during Communion last month. You two are able to express so much without words."

Alistair and I agreed to search for a suitable piece of music. We wanted the dance to be perfect

3

for our young friends, so we gave much thought and prayer to the choreography. The finished dance depicted a husband leading his wife to a deeper walk with Jesus. We spent hours perfecting every detail until the big day arrived. As the final notes of the performance died away and we turned to face the congregation, I saw tears in many eyes.

After the ceremony, the happy couple left the church in a shower of smiles and confetti. On the steps, an elderly lady rushed forward and grabbed my hand. "Oh, that was so beautiful. Your love for each other shone out from every movement. Oh, and at the end when Alistair lifted you high, gently lowered you, and then took your face in his hand and directed your gaze toward heaven? Well, it was just the loveliest thing. You two are such a blessing to this church."

ALISTAIR WAS OUT of town, choreographing for a small theatre company. I raced home from the ballet school after teaching the evening classes. My mother met me at the door, kissed me on the cheek, and told me our two small sons had eaten their dinner and were tucked in bed. I flew up the stairs, peeped into their rooms, and breathed a sigh of relief; they were fast asleep.

I quickly showered and changed my clothes. As I removed hairpins and shook my hair free, I heard voices in the lane. I gave up on fixing my

makeup and raced downstairs to greet the first of
our friends.

Visitors handed me plates of homemade
cookies and muffins before removing their heavy
coats and scarves. Even on the coldest night, the
welcoming charm of our old stone cottage drew
people in. Everyone relaxed in a favourite chair.
The rustle of pages, the soft rise and fall of voices,
and the crackle of the fire were the familiar sounds
of our Bible study.

Chatter and laughter during supper reached
such a pitch it woke the boys. I went upstairs to
settle them again, which took quite some time.
When I came down, everyone had gone home
except one friend who remained to clear the supper
things.

"It's lovely to come here and sit by the fire
with all your quaint old stuff about. It's an escape
from the real world. I envy you, you know, with
your beautiful home, your happy marriage." She
disappeared into the kitchen. "Where's the Cling
Wrap?"

"In the old pine cupboard to the right of the
fridge," I answered from the sitting room.

I carried the last things into the kitchen to find
her standing by the open cupboard door.

She looked up with a troubled expression. "I
didn't know you were drinkers."

My stomach twisted in a knot as I moved to
where I could see what she saw. Behind rolls of

paper towel and aluminium foil, almost hidden by a pile of paper serviettes, a half-empty bottle of rum lay on its side.

My reply came too quickly, and my heart sank. "Left over from the Christmas cake." Would she guess my secret?

Alistair was an alcoholic. But I smiled and pretended everything was normal. For in our church, people with problems—even small problems such as an untidy house or rebellious children—were judged as spiritual failures. If Alistair's alcohol problem became common knowledge… well, that did not bear thinking about.

As I ushered my friend to the door, I kept up a steady stream of pleasant chatter. Once she was gone, I closed the door and leaned against it, wondering how long I could keep living this charade.

A charade that had begun years before…

During our courtship, when we were both in our early twenties, I sometimes thought I detected a faint odour of alcohol about this man I loved. While warming up for a performance one evening, I was certain I smelled it on his breath. Not sure how to raise the subject, I teased him about it.

He laughed. "Mouthwash—I'm just being considerate!" He kissed me and continued with his warm-up. Watching him move with such strength and ease, it seemed impossible he had been drinking, but uneasiness lingered in the pit of my stomach.

Though I kept a close eye on him, never once did I see anything out of the ordinary. At opening night parties where the champagne flowed, he drank orange juice. I convinced myself I was just being silly. He loved me, I loved him, and a diamond sparkled on my left hand. What on earth was I worrying about?

We had been married for only a few months when, searching for a lost earring, I found a bottle hidden under the seat of his car. That was the first of many such discoveries. Our fairy tale marriage became a nightmare. I begged him to stop drinking, to seek help. He promised he would, but time and time again he broke his promises.

An old friend suggested we come to church with her. Though reluctant at first, I agreed to go, thinking it might help Alistair. Yet Sunday after Sunday, my own heart was stirred. The words of a song or the scripture reading seemed to be just for me.

I looked forward to Sunday. I longed for the joy and peace I saw in the faces of those around me but was struck with my unworthiness. This was something I'd never experienced before. I had always considered myself to be a good person, yet this feeling of shame would not go away.

As we left the church one Sunday morning, my friend slipped a gospel tract into my hand. Only a few weeks before, I would have dropped that booklet straight in the rubbish bin, but now I held onto it as though it were a precious treasure.

I did not read it right away but waited until late in the evening when I could be alone. When I got to, "For all have sinned and fall short of the glory of God" (Romans 3:32 NIV), I felt a pang of doubt. What if my goodness was not enough? Could this be why I felt unworthy? How could I be sure that if there were a heaven, I would go there?

I continued to read through the little book. "For God so loved the world that He gave His one and only Son so that whoever believes in Him will not perish but have eternal life" (John 3:16 NIV). I struggled to understand. What did it mean to believe in Jesus? Did it mean to believe that He lived once, two thousand years ago, or was there more? I went to bed with no answers.

The next morning, I called my friend and asked her to come over. Tenderly, she led me to understand that to believe in Jesus meant to put my trust in Him. She told me that no one is good enough to stand before God. We could not make it to heaven if Jesus had not taken the punishment we deserve. Jesus paid the price for my freedom. And that, she said, is what I had to trust in to be sure of eternal life.

"He's been reaching out to you all your life, and He is reaching out to you now. If you ask Him, He'll bring to your mind specific things for which you need to ask His forgiveness. If nothing comes to mind, simply tell Him you are sorry you have ignored Him all these years and, most important of all, thank Him for paying for your freedom with His life."

I poured it all out with tears, words tumbling over each other, until stillness filled my heart. Then, as my friend led me, I prayed that Jesus would come into my innermost being and be Lord of my life.

I felt a joyous release. I knew I was forgiven, loved, and accepted by the One who loves perfectly. Within me was undeniable new life. "Born again" was a term I had heard, but now I knew what it meant.

I felt as though I had not lived until that moment. The strength of the certainty that I was loved and forgiven was like a light inside, transforming everything and filling me with joy. I tried to tell Alistair about it but could not adequately express the feeling of release and renewal. It was beyond words.

A few Sundays later, after the service, I noticed Alistair speaking with the minister, and then they slipped into the office. I hoped he would tell the minister everything. But when we drove home, he said nothing about it, and I didn't press him.

The next morning, Alistair left with the ballet company for an extended tour. I stayed home, as I was expecting our first child. That evening, Alistair called from his hotel room to tell me what he had been unable to say face-to-face: he had accepted Jesus as his saviour.

I was overjoyed. If he felt as I did, his drinking problem would be a thing of the past. But once he returned home from the tour, it soon became obvious that little had changed. I continued to find bottles. Each time, he tearfully asked my forgiveness and promised not to drink. But there was always another bottle.

The artistic director of the ballet company became aware of my husband's drinking problem and terminated his contract. We opened a ballet school together and picked up extra work choreographing for small theatre companies and teaching in schools. But once the demands of dancing professionally were gone, Alistair's drinking problem became worse.

I went to our minister and told him everything. He and his wife were discreet and supportive. They prayed with my husband and arranged for him to have counselling, making sure he attended Alcoholics Anonymous. But the pattern continued: broken promises, repentance, more broken promises.

Around the time our second son was born, a sweet move of the Holy Spirit swept through our small congregation. The joy was contagious, transforming lives and bringing many to the Lord. Our small church grew rapidly. A larger building

was required, and that soon filled to capacity.
During those exciting years we saw miraculous
answers to prayer and a number of dramatic
healings. But not everyone was healed. My husband
was not one of the blessed ones, and I wondered
why.

As word of the church's revival spread, many
people came from other churches, bringing new
ideas. These newcomers said those who were not
healed "lacked faith" or were "in secret sin." Books
on prayer and spiritual warfare circulated through
the congregation. These books claimed that if
prayers were to be answered, special phrases and
verses of scripture must be spoken, and both the
person being prayed for and the one praying must
be without sin. Our minister tried to stem the flow
of these ideas, but he could not prevent them from
growing and taking hold. What began as a trickle
soon became a flood.

Our minister and a large number of the
original congregation left, but we stayed. This new
teaching made sense to me. There had to be a
reason my prayers remained unanswered. Maybe I
hadn't been praying the right words. Could I be in
sin and not know it? I inspected my life for things
that might be amiss. I stopped going to the cinema
and gave up choreographing Jazz Ballet. I had less
contact with friends outside the church.

With the arrival of a new minister, the focus
and teaching of the church swung towards the

extreme. He preached that a Christian's birthright was health and wealth; suffering came only to those who were not right with God. Weekend seminars taught us the right way to pray. There seemed to be so many rules.

Only a couple of close friends knew of my husband's problems, and they had left the church. Those who remained saw us as the ideal couple, the beautiful dancers with the beautiful home and the beautiful children.

Alistair made it easy to keep up this illusion. He attended church every Sunday and participated in the men's group and Bible studies, apparently a committed Christian. Always genuinely loving and attentive toward me and our two little sons, he was, in every respect bar one, the model husband. He never slurred his words or became violent or silly. His tolerance of alcohol was so high even I found it hard to tell if he had been drinking. His poise rarely wavered, and he was never without his peppermints. Money missing from our bank account, my purse, or the ballet school cash drawer was the only sure indicator he was drinking heavily.

I would confront him; he would deny it. I would yell, he would cry and ask me to forgive him. He would assure me he had been "trying so hard" and had been "dry for weeks but slipped up just this once." The scene repeated over and over.

∽

ALISTAIR COULD NOT bring himself to admit the extent of his problem. He wanted to be sober; he wanted me to think he was sober. He wanted my respect and the respect of the church, yet he simply could not beat this thing. I loved him dearly and saw his pain. I longed to help my precious man escape the clutches of addiction. Years of prayer and fasting as the church taught brought no release, yet I did not give up hope. I firmly believed it was only a matter of continuing in prayer. God would heal my husband. I had no doubt.

Edith Harrington

∽

Chapter 2

∽

The Illusion Crumbles

MY MUSCLES ACHED. Saturday was a long, exhausting day when Alistair was away, for I taught every class without a break. After the luxury of a long bath, I snuggled into bed. I took the pillows from Alistair's side and propped myself up. Tonight I could read as long as I wanted; he wouldn't be home until Sunday evening.

Some time later, I woke with a start. The light was still on, and my book lay open where it had fallen. A car started and accelerated quickly, its note droning off into the distance. I turned off the light, rolled over, and fell into a deep sleep.

The alarm woke me. I threw back the covers and hurried out of bed. Getting two little boys dressed in time for church is a struggle for two parents. On my own, it seemed to take three times as long.

"Quickly boys, hop in the car. If we don't hurry, we'll be late."

David, my elder son, jumped from the back seat to the front to play driving as I buckled up Peter. "Look, Mummy, there's a letter on the steering wheel!"

Even from the back seat I recognized my husband's writing. How could this be? Wasn't he miles away? Then I remembered hearing a car driving off in the middle of the night.

Hands trembling, I pulled the note from the steering wheel and read it. My throat tightened, and the boys' chatter seemed to come from a far distance. I was alone with my fear.

"I have been drinking again and no longer want to put you through the heartache."

This had the sound of a suicide note.

Frantic, I called the company he had gone to work with the day before, only to be told that he had not worked with them for months. I then called anyone and everyone who might know where he could be. Finally, I reported him missing with the police. I desperately prayed he was safe.

Days passed into weeks with no clue. Night after night, my little boys cried for their daddy and asked where he was, when he was coming back. I tried to comfort them, holding them close. Their sobs tore at my own pain, making it almost unbearable. I longed to make the empty promise that daddy would be home soon, anything to ease their fears.

Students and parents whispered about Alistair's sudden disappearance. Gossip quickly spread to the wider community, and it wasn't long before the truth was uncovered. My husband had run off with another woman, who had left her husband and children. Pain shredded my heart.

But there was more to come.

In a city as small as ours, it's hard to keep anything a secret. Yet I had never heard an inkling of his philandering before, though for the rest of the community, it was common knowledge. With Alistair gone, people came forward to tell me what they knew. First the lady at our corner shop, then my hairdresser. Shock followed shock, blow after blow. I would still be trying to come to terms with one startling revelation when another would hit me.

At first I couldn't accept what I was hearing. It seemed unbelievable, a soap-opera plot—yet the stories verified each other. As the pieces came together, I could no longer deny the obvious. My husband had been living a double life from the very beginning of our marriage. The affairs were so numerous he must have moved straight from one conquest to another with no break in between.

One final blow sent me reeling. Some of those affairs had been with men.

I thought I knew him. During all the years of dancing together, I never suspected this! Waiting weeks for results of an AIDs test was agonizing. I thanked God when I finally learned it was clear.

Pain engulfed me, consumed me. I struggled to comprehend the scope of the deception. My life was an unfamiliar landscape, and I was lost in it. Nothing was as I'd thought, and even happy memories were now tainted. Gnawing pain made it impossible to sleep. Night after night I sat alone in the dark.

The crackle of the fire and its soft glow usually brought some comfort, but one night I noticed the firelight reflecting on our family photos. Our smiling faces seemed to mock me. In reality, the happy life those photos showed had never existed. Our whole marriage had been a lie. Anger fuelled by grief welled up. One by one I removed each photo from its frame and burnt it. With shaking hands I pulled the albums from the bookcase and did not stop until every memento of our years together had been consigned to the flames.

On those sleepless nights, my thoughts whirled with endless questions. I asked myself how I could have been so blind. How could I have lived with him all these years and not seen, not suspected? Those questions filled me with self-doubt. Other questions brought doubt of a different kind, doubt that tore at the very fabric of my faith.

Why had God allowed this to happen? Where did I go wrong? Could I have done more? Should I have prayed more, fasted longer? Was there some key or formula I had missed? Nothing made sense anymore. I had no faith to pray, for prayer now seemed futile. I longed for God, for the trust and the certainty I had once known, but that had all slipped away beyond my reach. I balanced on a tiny square of faith. My one piece of solid ground was that Jesus had died for me, that I was saved. Beyond that fact lay an abyss of nothingness.

Because I could no longer trust God, I felt overwhelming guilt. Doubt and guilt were twin enemies who stalked me day and night.

I dragged myself into the studio and tried to teach as though everything were normal. I had to keep going. Teaching was my only income, and my husband had left many debts— including a personal loan I'd known nothing about.

After classes one evening, two elders from our church came to see me. Over coffee, I poured out my pain and shock at learning of my husband's secret life. Shaking, I told them of the alcoholism, the numerous affairs, the homosexuality, the stealing and lies.

As I spoke, I sensed their growing impatience, until one of the elders interrupted. "Well, we've heard of what Alistair has supposedly done; now, where do you fit into all this? What part did you play?"

They made it clear they thought I was lying, that I was to blame for my husband's leaving. I felt sick, as if they had physically struck me. Alistair had played his part too well. They couldn't believe that kind, caring Alistair could have done those terrible things. Cruel innuendo and ignorant assumptions followed.

My mind struggled to comprehend what they were suggesting. I was overwhelmed, mute and powerless to stop the flow of their soft, smiling superiority. Huge sobs escaped despite my efforts to keep them in.

Once the elders had gone, I collapsed into bed but did not sleep. Staring at the ceiling, all the sordid details of my husband's secret life swirled through my mind, mixed with repetitions of those men's words. "What part did you play? Where are you in all this?"

Mountainous waves of pain and despair rose and broke over me till I had to cry out, "Why, God, did You let this happen? What more could I have done?"

The elders publicly labelled me "out of the will of God." People who had previously been friends now avoided me. It was painful to see the ease with which they wiped me from their lives. Their gossip and rejection stripped away the last vestige of my confidence.

I had lost my husband and my financial security, my little boys had lost their daddy, and now, at the hands of my own church, I had lost my credibility. I felt worthless, a failure. Shame made me hide when I saw people from my church in the street. Why was I ashamed? I didn't know. I had done nothing wrong, yet I could not face them. I was afraid.

The black waters of depression rose steadily. I slipped beneath the surface, unaware of my descent until I lay in the depths of a silent well submerged in grief. No light could penetrate; the world outside was dull and hollow. Every effort to clamber out of that dark well only caused me to slip further toward the bottom. There were no finger grips, no toeholds. I was trapped.

Each day I woke exhausted, drained of energy. Getting out of bed took every ounce of grit I could muster. Shopping or going to the bank were now frightening experiences. Sudden panic attacks would seize me, sweating and shaking, in their grip. On one occasion, terror sent me running from the supermarket, leaving the trolley full of groceries in the aisle. Home became the only place I felt safe, and it became increasingly difficult to go out the door. Even in the ballet studio, waves of panic swamped me.

The simplest task was overwhelming. The sight of a pile of washing or a sink full of dishes brought nausea. I found it hard to steady my hand to write. Simple forms seemed incomprehensible, as if written in hieroglyphics. I felt I was going mad, yet I knew I must not go completely under, that at all costs I must keep going. I would practice relaxation techniques and control my breathing, steadying my nerves as I would before a performance, but even these familiar techniques often failed me.

My doctor said I was suffering from Post-Traumatic Stress Disorder and prescribed anti-depressants. I didn't want to take the tablets, but I was desperate, so reluctantly began the medication. The anti-depressants helped, but the blackness went deeper than my physical body. At its core was my loss of trust in God, and with that loss of trust came an intense fear of the future.

God had been the very centre of my life. Now that I could not trust Him, I had no centre. I carried an aching emptiness within, and I was lost in it. With the debts my husband left and my income effectively halved, I could not afford professional counselling. I stumbled along, somehow getting through each day. In the blackest times, I prayed, "O Lord, take me home. Please take me home. I cannot go on."

But I had to go on. I had my boys to care for. I would protect them. I would not let anything hurt them. And I would not be deceived again, ever!

Not even those closest to me knew how ill I was, for somehow I continued teaching, smiling, acting, mechanically doing all that was necessary to manage the ballet school and care for my boys. No one would have guessed that behind the smiles was an emptiness that consumed every ray of light.

I wandered from church to church, desperately searching for what I had lost—the sense of the

Lord's presence. But churches held rows and rows of people, and people now frightened me. Behind all those smiling faces might lie judgment to pierce my heart.

For months at a time I did not go to church. I was too afraid. And then, after two years of wandering, I found an old church where the people hardly noticed me—and for that, I was grateful. I went to services and nodded a polite good morning, but I did not let anyone get too close. Sunday after Sunday I sat, carefully dressed, poised, and controlled—but underneath, desperately lonely, frightened, and ill.

The minister of this church was a godly man. His preaching was a pure exposition of the Word, inspired and inspiring and full of God's love. The reverence and stillness within the thick stone walls of that church comforted me. The quiet, ordered structure was restful, and the words of the mighty hymns of our forefathers stirred the depths of my spirit, bringing up tiny fragments of my lost faith. But my deep longing for God was not met. A door inside my heart was locked. Not only could I not find the key, I could not find the door.

∽

Chapter 3

∽

But a Princess I Was Not

WITHIN A YEAR and a half of Alistair's disappearance, the gossip mill had done the work of
locating him for me. Many people were glad his lies
were finally uncovered, and some came to me with
information. My divorce lawyer was then able to
contact him. He agreed to end our marriage with a
generous settlement that enabled me to keep our
home and the ballet studio.

Once all was finalized, I bunkered down, filling
my days with work, trying to claw my way back to
financial security.

Then, at the beginning of the third year, I
stumbled into love. A chance meeting, unexpected
and unsought.

James was cultured, well-travelled, and well-
read. He courted me in style: dozens of long-
stemmed roses, exquisite poetry, and candlelight
dinners. It was so lovely to be loved, to feel special.
He called himself a Christian. I suspected his

Christianity was purely social convention, but my heart was swept up in the romance, and I brushed my suspicions aside.

When he proposed to me in the most romantic fashion, ending with a quote from Ecclesiastes 9:9 (TLB): "Live happily with the woman you love through the fleeting days of life, for the wife God gives you is your best reward down here for all your earthly toil," I accepted.

The pressure to keep going had drained the love of dance from me. Now, there was no need to keep struggling on. I felt I had been rescued. We married and moved to a large house in the country. My boys, then seven and ten, played hide-and-seek in the acres of beautiful gardens and returned muddy and happy after hours of exploring. I felt like a princess who had found her prince.

But a princess I was not. I was broken inside, suffering from crippling depression and panic attacks. I had played the role of ballerina princess during our courtship, but it was hard to maintain the poise twenty-four hours a day.

I believed that with my new husband's love and protection I would get better, but he was no more my rescuer prince than I was a princess. A senior person in the legal profession, James remained locked in his book-lined study most nights till the early hours of the morning. The attention I so desperately craved never came.

James had been married when he was much younger, but for most of his life he had been on his own. Cloistered away with his books, eating every meal in restaurants, he'd long dreamed of a family and a real home. Now that it was a reality, he was overjoyed. But I was overwhelmed. Maintaining a household of this size was like running a boutique hotel. Even with domestic help, the workload swamped me. But James, consumed by the pressures of his profession, remained oblivious to my distress.

Being naturally gregarious and now revelling in the novelty of being able to entertain at home, he enjoyed inviting people to dinner or to stay overnight. He expected I would easily manage the frenetic pace of his lifestyle. Having seen my ballet school and the organization it involved, he thought I'd entertain his friends and professional associates with ease. However, I'd spent every evening of my life in the ballet studio and knew little about cooking. I now studied cookbooks in desperation.

I became embroiled in a constant stream of dinner parties and houseguests. Almost every weekend, the house was full of people—wealthy, influential ones. I kept smiling and pretending, somehow pulling off act after act.

My family and friends thought I had a fairy tale life: living in a large country house, the boys now attending private school, traveling overseas for luxury holidays, driving a Rolls Royce, living in a whirl of parties and friends. But for me, it was a nightmare that rolled all my fears into one: crowds, strange places, and the pressure to keep it all together. I lived in a constant state of distress: acting, always acting, struggling to appear normal.

Eighteen months after our wedding, Claire was born. She was James' delight, his much-longed-for only child. But she did not sleep well. A combination of sleeplessness, running around collecting my boys from school and sports, midweek entertaining, and hosting weekend house parties, stretched me to the breaking point.

James would often phone late in the afternoon to say he was bringing people home to dinner. As we lived far from any store, I had to make sure the pantry and fridge were always stocked and ready for such eventualities.

Claire was nine months old when, late one afternoon, he called to say he was bringing a judge and his associate home for dinner. Something inside me snapped. I was gripped with panic. I couldn't remember how to prepare a meal. I screamed into the phone, "You can't! You can't!" and burst into hysterical tears.

He said, "What on earth is the matter with you? Pull yourself together. I have already invited them."

I shrieked in panic, "Make some excuse. If you bring them home, I won't be here!"

I hung up and fell to the ground, crippled by uncontrollable crying and shaking. After several minutes, the thought forced itself to the surface: "I'm sick. I need help."

I pulled myself to my feet and called my doctor. She saw me immediately, diagnosed Postnatal Depression, and confirmed what I already knew: I had never recovered from the Post Traumatic Stress Disorder. She gave me another prescription for anti-depressants and suggested I seek counselling.

Now that I had a diagnosis, I was sure James would give me understanding and support. But no, as I began to tell him about my depression, he held up his hand, signalling me to stop. "This is all nonsense. You don't need counselling, and you don't need those tablets. I do not want to see you take them, and I do not want to hear you speak of this again." With that he turned, went to his study, and shut the door. The study door wasn't the only one to close that night. The door of James' heart shut with a resounding thud, the echoes of which lingered for many months.

Until that day, I had managed reasonably well to disguise my symptoms. To him, I was a competent, accomplished woman. He simply could not understand what had happened to me. He convinced himself that I was just overtired and all I needed was to get a grip on myself.

The anti-depressants helped somewhat, but shaking, gut-wrenching fear was ever-present. I could barely function now. I seemed to be hanging onto my sanity by a thin thread, one which could break at any moment. I longed for my husband to understand, to put his arms around me and tell me that he loved me, that everything would be all right, but he never did. When I tried to explain, he made light of my situation. If I demanded a break from all the visitors, he would tell me to pull myself together and stop making a scene.

Why couldn't he see how ill I was? What was wrong with him? Why couldn't he give me the understanding I needed? I swung wildly between anger and despair, and in between times, I felt overwhelming guilt. I was a failure as a Christian, a failure as a wife, a failure as a mother. I was hardly aware of what I was doing. Days were a blur, and often I would even forget what day it was. I stumbled from one blunder to another, with my confidence steadily falling. I made lists and lists of lists but couldn't bring my life under control.

At night, I would creep into my sons' rooms and pray desperately for them. But these were prayers of panic, not prayers of faith. What would become of my sons? Would they inherit a predisposition for addiction from their father? Would they be forever scarred by his sudden disappearance, my depression, and a stepfather who gave them so little time? I prayed, but my words seemed lost in the vastness of the cosmos. Despair drove me to think, "What is the use of praying? I prayed before—I trusted and believed—and it was all for nothing." God seemed distant and indifferent.

∽

Chapter 4

∽

Old Books and Afternoon Tea

OUR LITTLE CLAIRE, now eighteen months old, played on the floor of my doctor's waiting room. The electric fan did little to relieve the midsummer heat.

My doctor's waiting room, like most others, seemed to be the last resting place of tacky magazines, dog-eared and years out of date. I regretted I had not brought a book.

The minutes dragged. The back of my legs stuck to the vinyl chair. I could stand it no longer and rummaged through the magazines on the table in front of me for something to read.

A decision of a moment—to reach forward and search—an ordinary thing. Yet it was not ordinary, for it was the first moment of a search that would lead to recovery, restoration, and faith.

I pulled a copy of *This England* magazine from the untidy pile, its cover worn and creased. I peered at the date. Twenty years old? Could it have been sitting here for two decades? Nostalgia and old houses were more to my liking than the usual waiting room fare, and I settled back for a good read.

A four-page article about a writer named Flora Klickman captivated me. Snippets from her books lifted me away to her cottage in Wales. I longed to escape inside the pages.

The article contained a list of her titles published between 1914 and 1930. By the time the doctor called my name, I had scribbled that list on a scrap of paper but then, in a last-minute act of bravery, I asked the doctor if I could keep the magazine. She agreed, and I could not wait to get home. I was determined to find copies of those books.

The moment I was inside my front door, I grabbed the Yellow Pages and turned to antiquarian booksellers. Phone in hand, I worked my way down the page. One by one they told me no, they had nothing by that author.

By the last call I was despondent, but this time a cheery male voice said, "Yes, I have three in stock." Quickly the transaction was completed. I gave my address and then, as an afterthought, he said, "There's another lady in your area who collects Flora Klickman. You should give her a call. She might have some doubles she'd be willing to sell." Then he told me her name.

What a coincidence! I had met the woman briefly years before and knew she was a Christian. As soon as I said good-bye to the dealer, I called Kaye. She was delighted that I was interested in Flora Klickman. And yes, she did have doubles— that she would *give*, not sell me. Right from that first phone call, we shared a special connection.

Kaye introduced me to her close friend, Dianna. Both of these godly women had suffered, yet there was no trace of bitterness about them. I felt safe with them. I could trust them.

They invited me to their afternoon teas, where I met more of their friends. These women, some young, some old, came from widely different backgrounds and churches. They were drawn together by their love for old Christian literature— and by their love for Kaye.

With a passion for vintage clothing from the '40s and '50s, Kaye had a gracious style all her own. She was petite and pretty, and her soft-spoken manner instantly put the listener at ease. In fact, all the women who met at Kaye's had an indefinable quality about them. It was as though, being so long immersed in old Christian writings, their faith had absorbed a trusting, quiet simplicity. Just being with them brought me peace. There was no striving, no demands, and, best of all, no judgment. I felt loved and accepted. Kaye, her dear sister Julia, and the other ladies took me into their hearts. With friends who didn't condemn me as a failure when I shared my problems, I did not have to pretend. I could relax and simply be myself.

Over the years, Kaye had amassed a horde of precious junkshop finds. Her bookshelves bulged with volumes large and small. The works of little-known writers jostled for shelf space with the greats of Christian literature. Whether in faded cloth covers or original dust-jackets, whether leather-bound and gilt-edged or held together with tape or string, the spiritual treasure these books held still shone.

With a knack for knowing just which book to lend, Kaye had a ministry. At first she loaned me the uplifting little books by H. L. Gee, who led me on walking tours through the English countryside with tender parables at every turn. Fay Inchfawn's *The House of Life* was next, deeply spiritual but homely and comforting.

How wise Kaye was! I could not have absorbed anything heavier than these simple delights. Years of "victory" and "prosperity" had made me feel a total failure. Most modern Christian books had only added to my feelings of guilt and inadequacy. In my search for help I had devoured psychology books, both Christian and secular. They offered practical counselling but didn't touch my heart. These old books were different. Through them, I began to catch a fresh glimpse of Jesus' love.

Each of Kaye's friends had her own collection. Swapping, laughing, and relating stories of the latest find were part of most gatherings. If they found a copy of something they had at home, they would buy it anyway and pass it on. Kaye gave me many of her doubles. I had always loved antiques and was no stranger to junk shops, but now I scrounged around in second-hand bookshops and searched through boxes at the prime pickings of church jumble sales. Rare editions can be found online with a click of the mouse, but it's such fun to get down on hands and knees among dusty shelves.

Taking turns to host tea parties, we dressed in our best clothes and set the table with our finest linen and china. We feasted on bite-sized sandwiches and scones piled high with jam and cream while discussing old books. We chatted, laughed, and prayed. Little by little, in spite of my crippling depression, I was comforted by the timeless books and the dear friends who gave me such unconditional love.

After some months, Kaye loaned me an old daily devotional. *Springs in the Valley* by Mrs. Charles E. Cowman, a much-loved junk shop treasure of Kaye's. It had blessed her, and she felt it would be a help to me. Each day as I read those soothing entries, the tenderness and love of Jesus flowed into my deep wounds like cool water and soothing ointment. Gentle and encouraging, the faith of our forefathers spoke to my heart as no modern Christian writings had. This old book did not try to explain the reason for suffering. It simply accepted suffering as a fact that is normal for a follower of the Man of Sorrows. I found it restful, so restful.

I developed the habit of copying into a notebook the readings that were meaningful to me. Soon I established a regular pattern in my quiet times: reading the daily portion, writing, and praying. Little by little I began, not just to copy out the passage, but also to write about what the readings meant to me and to record some of my prayers.

∽

Chapter 5

∽

Stones and Iron, Brass and Hills

ON NEW YEAR'S Day, a little over a year after meeting Kaye, I sat with the old devotional propped open on my knee, copying out the reading for the day. This portion of scripture touched me, as it held a promise of better things to come in the New Year.

> For the Lord thy God bringeth thee into a good land, a land of brooks of water, of fountains and depths that spring out of valleys and hills; A land of wheat and barley and vines and fig trees and pomegranates. A land of olive oil and honey. A land wherein thou shalt eat bread without scarceness. Thou shalt not lack anything in it; a land whose stones are iron, and out of whose hills thou mayest dig brass. When thou hast eaten and art full, then thou shalt bless the LORD thy God

for the good land which He hath given thee." (Deuteronomy 8:7-10 KJV)

Verse 9 held my attention: "A land whose stones are iron and out of whose hills thou mayest dig brass."

There was nothing in that verse to hold me, and yet it did. I wondered what it meant.

The literal, historical meaning of the passage was plain: God would bring Israel into their own country as promised, with its fertile soil and its land rich with minerals. But the scriptures have a spiritual application as well. It was the gentle prompting of the Holy Spirit that called me to search for the deeper, spiritual meaning.

The devotional explained that the *brooks of water* and the *fountains* represented the infinite sources of God's blessing through His word to us, refreshing, satisfying our thirst. *Bread* spoke of Jesus Himself, the Bread of Life. The author said *a land of plenty; bread without scarceness* meant God's abundant supply. *Olive oil* represented the beautiful Holy Spirit, and *honey*, the sweetness of His love. *Pomegranates*, being a fruit bursting with seeds, represented a life that reproduced itself in the blessing of others.

But for verse 9, the book offered no explanation.

I found myself thinking about that verse over the next several days. *Whose stones are iron and out of whose hills thou mayest dig brass.* It was tantalizing. I knew there was more to this verse, but weeks passed with the meaning still just beyond reach. Until...

Just after midnight, I awoke. I tried to settle back to sleep, but those words *whose stones are iron and out of whose hill thou mayest dig brass* came creeping. I had woken before to find them running through my mind, hinting, calling, and keeping me from sleep. I couldn't go on like this, so I prayed, "Lord, please, if this is important to me, would You show me what it means?"

The Holy Spirit seemed to whisper, "What are stones?"

I thought for a moment, and the answer formed in my mind. Stones are common. They are found lying on the ground everywhere. Sometimes we trip over them, kick our toe against them, or they cut our feet. Some are so big they seem impossible to get around. Others are quite small, but they can get in our shoe and cause us to walk with a limp. Some are as tiny as a grain of sand, but as they rub over and over on the same tender spot, they become too much to bear.

I gasped. Of course! Stones represent the common everyday problems, irritations, and aggravations of life. No one can escape them, for they are everywhere. We each have our own particular stones.

Then, as if a veil lifted, I became aware that the items on the list in Deuteronomy 8:7-10—water, bread, olive oil etc.—were all blessings of the Promised Land. And, with a dream-like sense of wonder, it dawned upon me that stones are on the list.

Could stones be blessings? Mine were still with me in spite of continued prayer. Could God be allowing them to remain because they had a purpose?

I thought back over each of the other blessings in those verses:

Water, the symbol of the Word of God, baptism, renewal and forgiveness.

Bread, the symbol of Jesus Himself.

Olive oil, the symbol of the Holy Spirit.

Each item in the list is a precious gift. But what gift did the stones give? What was their blessing?

The verse said, "The stones are iron." Was the blessing something to do with iron?

Then I remembered that iron is the biblical symbol for strength. Therefore, "stones are iron" must mean "stones are strength."

Strength was the gift of the stones?

These stones that caused me so much pain, these very things, were to strengthen me? How could that be? They didn't give strength; they drained me!

It seemed impossible, but there was a quiet insistence deep in my spirit.

I thought again about those words, "Whose stones are iron." The statement was emphatic, definite. The stones *are* iron.

The stones are strength.

I found it hard to comprehend, but there in the stillness, I felt the Lord leading me deeper into this truth.

Stones listed among the great blessings of the Promised Land?

Yes, they were there—bread, water, olive oil, and stones symbolizing Jesus, the Word of God, the Holy Spirit, and...*difficulties!*

I lay awake, but I did not feel tired. I heard the grandfather clock in the downstairs hall strike two, and then what seemed like moments later, three, as I pondered *"And out of whose hills thou mayest dig brass."* It meant nothing to me.

In the stillness, the Holy Spirit whispered a second question. "What is a hill?" And again, as I lay staring into the blackness, the answer formed in my mind.

A hill requires a steep upward climb, a sustained effort to reach the top.

In *Pilgrims Progress*, John Bunyan called big problems "Hill Difficulty." That which is not attained in a day.

I was climbing my Hill Difficulty. Others had their own to climb: hills of sickness, loss, breakdown of marriage, big problems that go on day after day. These are not the small difficulties stones represent. These problems are long and steep.

I drew breath and sat up in my bed, incredulous. Hills had brought me nothing but sorrow, and all my energy had been directed at praying against them. But hills are in that list of the eternal blessings.

For some minutes I pondered the implications of this: my struggles with the ordinary circumstances of life were my stones, and depression was the hill I must climb.

That revelation seemed to hang in the air. Then, like an insistent drum beat, "Out of whose hills thou mayst dig brass" returned.

We may dig brass? What on earth did *that* mean?

Moments passed. I waited, wondering, and then another question formed in my mind. What is brass?

The answer came quickly. Brass is a yellow metal that looks like gold.

Brass looks like gold?

I saw the connection. Gold represents spiritual truth. Brass looks like gold, but brass tarnishes. To keep brass shining, it needs to be regularly polished.

I crept out of bed silently so as not to wake James, and went downstairs to the ironing room where I kept my notebook and the old devotional. I opened the battered notebook, slowly turning the pages back through the months of scripture, quotes, and poems. With a new awareness, the beauty of each returned.

When I'd recorded them, those precious truths had shone like gold. I thought I would never forget the lift they had given my spirit. But I had forgotten them. They had tarnished.

The lesson was obvious: brass represents spiritual insights that must be constantly revisited to keep them shining and vital, to be spiritual gold.

I had heard the phrase "nuggets of truth," so I decided to call each new insight from the Holy Spirit a nugget of brass. I prayed that I might not allow one of these precious nuggets to tarnish.

By then, it was almost dawn. I read the verse through again and noticed it said I *may* dig. As I climbed Hill Difficulty, I could choose whether or not to dig for brass that could be made to shine like gold. I had a choice.

I'd constantly felt guilty that I did not spend more time studying the Bible, but I just did not have the energy. Most days I fell into bed exhausted, with a few mumbled prayers.

Then the wonder of the next thought brought tears. The Lord knew I had no strength to dig. He had placed these nuggets of brass at my feet so I would be spared the effort of digging. The Lord had led my hand to the magazine that led me to Kaye, who gave me the devotional.

The sun's first rays spread across my garden, lifting delicate scarves of mist from the stream. Hope crept into my heart.

∽

Chapter 6

∽

Digging Nuggets, Polishing Brass

AFTER THAT NIGHT, I determined to believe that the Lord would use my stones—all the stressful demands of my life—and my hills—the symptoms of depression—to make me strong.

But still, most days, exhaustion and hopelessness crept up and flooded over me. Irrational fears held me in their grip, and I was powerless against them. I knew for me to move forward, it was important to keep trusting that these stones and hills had a purpose.

The problem was, I didn't understand how the stones could strengthen me, or the hills of difficulty bring forth gold. How could I ever move forward?

Brass Nugget 1: Hills

On a day when despair and hopelessness swept in, I reached for an old book Kaye had recently lent me. I flicked through the pages absentmindedly. I felt too low to read but looked down to where I had randomly stopped. At the top of the page was:

"The mountains will bring prosperity to the people and the hills the fruit of righteousness" (Psalm 72:3 WEB).

The mountains *will* bring prosperity… the hills righteousness.

I was held in awed stillness. In the past, I would have read that verse simply as a piece of lovely literature—poetic, but without practical implications. Now, as impossible as it seemed, I knew God was confirming that out of my steep mountains would come true spiritual prosperity, not the sort that prosperity teaching promised. I would become rich in the things of God. The Hills of Difficulty would bring into my life a righteousness that had nothing to do with lists of dos and don'ts.

As I tried to take it all in, another verse from the Psalms came to mind.

"I will lift up mine eyes unto the hills. From whence cometh my help? My strength cometh from the Lord" (Psalm 121:1-2, KJV).

A new light fell on this verse. If I kept looking at my Hills of Difficulty, I would feel I did not have the strength to face them. I would quake at the sight of them and fall back into that black well of despair. But if I looked to the Lord, He would give me the strength to keep climbing.

I wrote those verses in my notebook and added in large letters, "My strength comes from the Lord!"

Brass Nugget 2: And Again

Though it came through a strong revelation breathed by the Holy Spirit, living out the truth of "Stones are Iron" proved harder than expected. I'd thought the wonder of that night would somehow give me the strength to live in a new way. But six months passed, and I still struggled. One day up a little, the next down in the black waters.

Gently, the Lord led me to a new nugget.

I finished stacking the dishwasher, breathed a sigh of relief, and headed for the ironing room to begin my morning quiet time. This small room, which had once been a home office, had become my personal sanctuary.

As I removed my notebook from the over-crowded shelf, a music book fell to the ground and opened when it landed. It was the third time this book had fallen. Annoyed, I promised myself I would rearrange the shelves. As I picked it up this last time, I glanced at the page and realized that the last two times it fell, it had opened to that same place.

I sat down, the book open in my lap, and wondered at the chances of it falling open to the same place three times. I checked to see if the binding had been weakened so that it naturally opened to that page, but it wasn't. I held the book in wonder.

The song it opened to paraphrased the words of Jeremiah 31:3-6:

> I have loved you with an everlasting
> love.
> With mercy have I drawn you to me,
> And again I will build you,
> And you will be strong,
> O virgin of Israel.
> You shall be adorned with timbrels.
> With joy you shall go forth and dance.
> Let us go up to the mountain of Zion.
> Let us worship the Lord our God.[1]

With its reference to dance, this was a very familiar scripture to me. But two little words seemed to leap from the page.

"*And again*, I will build you and you will be strong."

Yes, once I had been strong, but that was like a dream. Could one so weak ever be strong again? Yet, there they were, those two little words, *and again*, and following them, the promise that the Lord Himself would build me and I would be strong.

I will be strong. I said those words over and over to myself, at first almost in disbelief. But the words *I will build you* shouted louder than my doubts and fears. The Lord had said that He would build me. Oh, I wish I could convey to you the wonder this was to me! I clung to those two little words like a life raft. "*And again* I will build you and you will be strong."

I shared this nugget with Kaye, Dianna, and Elizabeth, and they delighted in it with me. I shared it with another friend whose husband suffered from depression, and she wrote "AND AGAIN I will build you and you will be strong" in giant letters on large pieces of paper and stuck them up all round their house.

Every day, I spent time reading the old devotional and reviewing my notes, praying through the things the Lord had shown me. I always went back to Jeremiah 31:3-6. Its wonderful promise of rebuilding gave me strength.

But as the days passed, I became aware that when I read verse 3, "I have loved you with an everlasting love," an unsettling feeling would creep over me. I asked myself why. From somewhere deep within me, questions bubbled up.

How can God say He loves me when He has allowed all these stones in my life? These stones may be to strengthen me, but I can't see how. Surely, if God loved me, He would find another way to teach me and strengthen me.

Surely, if God loved me!

The root of my problem revealed itself. Deep down in the secret places of my heart, I did not believe God loved me. I did not trust Him for the future.

But how could I be expected to trust Him, considering all He had allowed in the past?

Scripture told me Jesus loved me, but I was not confident of that. I wanted to be, but I couldn't manufacture that assurance.

Some days, I seemed able to trust just a little, but any sudden stress or upset would push me down into that slippery-sided well once more. I seemed stuck in the mire until some months later, the Lord gave me the next brass nugget.

Brass Nugget 3: I Was With You

The weekend kept me busy, with guests in every bedroom. Then on Sunday afternoon, more friends gathered for lunch in the garden. On Monday, Ena, the lady who helped me in the house, called to say she couldn't come because her son was ill. There was much to do, and I didn't know where to start.

My jumbled thinking made it impossible to do things in an orderly fashion. When Ena was with me, she brought order and direction, and she had become one of my dearest friends. Without her, I seemed to run from one thing to another, accomplishing nothing.

As I battled with the breakfast clean-up, I pondered the scene in Luke 10:38-42 in which Martha worked frantically while Mary sat at Jesus' feet. My thoughts wandered—housework, serving, making time for the Lord. I finished the dishes and moved onto the vacuuming, my thoughts straying to the account of Jesus raising Lazarus.

I felt drawn to leave what I was doing, get my Bible, and read that portion of scripture. I tried to ignore the feeling, determined to discipline myself to finish one task before moving to another. But the prompting grew insistent, so I dropped the vacuum cleaner, raced to the ironing room, settled in my chair, and opened my Bible.

I'd read that passage, John 11:1-44, many times before, but this time was different. As I read, a deep stillness quietened my mind. Time seemed suspended… the scene unfolded. I sat with Mary and Martha, waiting. Minutes were like hours as their loved one hovered between life and death. They waited, but Jesus did not come. Despair gripped them… pain ripped open their hearts… it was too late…their brother lay dead.

I felt their anguish. I knew their questioning. "Where is Jesus?"

I understood their grief—the grief of the deserted.

Then I saw Jesus crying. His tears brought me comfort, though at first I was unable to say why. I held my breath as a new insight began to form in my mind.

Jesus had planned the resurrection of Lazarus as a joyous gift to those He loved.

He wanted more for His friends than the miracle of healing. He wanted them to have a foretaste of the resurrection. But that required that He wait, bide His time until death came.

Jesus knew how His dear friends suffered, believing He had failed them. The delay was agonizing for Him. He longed to rush to them and end their pain. When finally He came, His long-planned gift just moments away, Jesus could not contain His tears.

Though He knew the joyous ending, He felt their grief. Though He allowed their suffering, He was not insensitive to it.

As that truth slowly, so slowly, crept into my broken heart, the grief of the deserted was eased. I understood Jeremiah 31:3, "I have loved you." Jesus had loved me through all the lonely years when I thought He had forgotten me.

The words on the well-worn notebook page echoed the truth. "I have loved you with an everlasting love." The warmth of God's love washed over me. I closed my eyes and repeated it aloud. "I have loved you with an everlasting love."

And then with surprise I realized the verse looks both ways.

The past tense *I have loved you* looks back, while *with an everlasting love* looks forward to eternity. Jesus stands in the middle, His arms outstretched to touch both past and future.

Through all my suffering, Jesus had not stood far off, distant, impersonal. He had been with me through it all, watching and loving me, grieving with me, and offering comfort, though I had not perceived it.

And He would love me into the everlasting future.

∞

Chapter 7

∞

Baby Steps

THE LORD LED me graciously in tiny increments.

The steps were small, because He knew I was too weak to make great leaps of faith. I had to be led by the hand one baby step at a time. Some days I felt like giving up, and I doubted I had heard from God at all. Then gentle promptings and tender encouragements caught and lifted me.

One such encouragement came on a particularly bad day when I could not extract even an ounce of hope from *and again I will build you.* I sat at my desk feeling like a ruin that could never be rebuilt.

Slumped in my chair, my hand resting on the open devotional, I glanced down. My finger rested on the line "Begin to Build Anew."

The Lord spoke those words right into my heart, strengthening me. Then I read the prayer above it, written over a hundred years ago by Robert Louis Stevenson.

Help us with the grace of courage that
none of us be cast down while we sit
lamenting over the ruins of our happiness.
Touch us with the fire of Thine altar, that
we may be up and doing, to rebuild the
city. [2]

"The grace of courage to rebuild the city," I
repeated.

What were the chances of randomly opening
to that page? This was no coincidence.

I could again trust that I was not simply
deceiving myself. God would rebuild me.

In those few moments, God lifted me from
despair to hope. As I copied that prayer into my
notebook, I thought, "This is so precious and
tender, how could I doubt God is leading me?"
And yet, there were many days when I did doubt.

Brass Nugget 4: A Privilege

After the usual morning rush of organizing
James and the boys came the most peaceful time of
the day. I would settle Claire with her teddies in
front of the television to watch her favourite
DVDs—Angelina Ballerina or Peter Rabbit and
Friends—while I busied myself with household
chores. One morning, I resisted the temptation to
race about and clean up the mess, and opened my
Bible instead.

I read the first chapter of Philippians until

verse 29 stopped me. "For it has been granted to you on behalf of Christ not only to believe in him, but also to suffer for him" (NIV). The word *granted* seemed to leap off the page. "It has been *granted* to you… to suffer…" To be granted a thing is to be given a special favour. It implies privilege.

How could that be? My previous church saw suffering as a sign of being out of the will of God, having curses on your life, or being in sin. Though I still felt uncertain, I wrote that verse in my notebook, heavily underlining *granted*.

Brass Nugget 5: A Post of Honour

A few weeks later, a nugget in the old devotional built on the amazing thought that suffering is a special privilege.

"Endure hardship, as a good soldier of Jesus Christ" (2 Timothy 2:1 NKJV).

The commentary on this verse read:

> The post of honour in war is so called because it is attended by difficulties and dangers to which few are equal; yet generals usually allot these hard services to their favourites and friends, who on their part eagerly take them as tokens of favour and marks of confidence.

Should we not, therefore, account it an

honour and a privilege when the
Captain of our salvation assigns us a
difficult post?[3]

I found it hard to think of suffering as an
honour and a privilege. Suffering had made me feel
a failure as a Christian. This idea was totally foreign
to me.

Brass Nugget 6: Bread and Water

Though Isaiah 30:20 was a familiar scripture, it
jarred me one morning during my study time. It
was as though I had never seen the verse before.

"Though *He gives you* the bread of adversity and
water of affliction, yet He will be with you to teach
you—with your own eyes you will see your
Teacher" (TLB).

Adversity and affliction? Everything I had ever
been taught, everything I had believed, was just the
opposite of this. My head swam, but the list in my
notebook was growing.

- Stones develop strength.
- Dig into Hills of Difficulty to find spiritual
  treasure.
- Mary and Martha suffered. Jesus planned
  it, but he suffered with them.
- It has been *granted* me to suffer.
- Suffering is a privilege.
- Suffering is a post of honour.

I added to the list:

- Adversity will feed me.
- Affliction will satisfy my thirst for the deep things of God.
- Through this suffering, I will come to see God.

Brass Nugget 7: A Firm Foundation

The early morning stillness echoed with bird song. Light had not yet reached our valley, but the ridge tops glowed opalescent. I read through my notebook and stopped at the words, "And again I will build you."

I started to pray, but my thoughts wandered. I slipped comfortably into my favourite daydream of walking through the rooms of my old home, seeing them as they used to be: each piece of furniture, each picture in its place; my little boys asleep in their beds, the quilts I had so lovingly made covering them, all safe.

I still grieved for that old stone cottage with a longing deep and painful. It seemed to encompass all I had lost. But this time, the daydream took a new turn, back to the day when I first saw the house.

It had not been lived in for many years, and the smell of mould, neglect, and decay pervaded all. The roof leaked and most of the ceilings had fallen in, but the basic structure was surprisingly strong. Only one wall was unstable. I had hoped that wall would be easily fixed with a buttress, but when a builder closely examined the bulging sections, he said there was no option but to demolish the wall. Once all the stones were down, he declared the foundations were strong, and the wall could be rebuilt upon them.

I remembered vividly the demolition and rebuilding. Stone by stone the wall came down; stone by stone it was built up again. The re-building enabled the original small window to be enlarged into a bay window. Light flooded the room.

As I sat reminiscing, the symbolism quietly did its work. Instead of the usual sense of loss and poignant longing in remembering that house, there came peace. Could it be that out of the rubble of my life the Lord would rebuild *me*? Not restoring me to past strength, but to a totally new, light-filled life?

I whispered, "Lord, you are the foundation of my life. I want to trust You. But this pulling down hurts so much."

∞

Chapter 8

∞

More Baby Steps

Brass Nugget 8: The Master Jeweller

THE CHILDREN WERE asleep, and James, locked in his study, wrestled with a difficult legal matter. It had been a hard day—one in a long series of hard days. I turned out the lights downstairs and, though it was still only 8:30 p.m., prepared for bed.

I sat propped up in bed reading the Bible. When I came to Isaiah 54:11, "[Thou] afflicted, tossed with tempest, not comforted!" I lowered my head, overcome by waves of exhaustion and emptiness.

Afflicted, tossed with tempest, not comforted. That was me, for sure. Oh, how I longed for the comfort of the simple, trusting faith I had once known. It had been so easy then, when everything made sense. Now there seemed to be little comfort.

Tears ran down my nose and dripped onto my Bible. I thought, "No, I can't go back. I can only keep going forward even if it makes no sense."

I lifted my head and continued to read: "I will set your stones in antimony to enhance their brilliance."

My tears blurred the words. As my focus cleared, the word "stones" took shape on the page. The now-familiar stirring of the Holy Spirit brought stillness and an inner listening.

A jeweller sets gemstones with great care to make beautiful adornments: rings, necklaces, even crowns. Could the Lord take my rough stones, transform them into precious gems, and set them in a crown?

But then another question floated to the surface. *What is this antimony in which He will set them? And how will it enhance their brilliance?*

With sudden enthusiasm, I jumped out of bed and ran downstairs to the ironing room, where I pulled a few different translations from the bookshelf. But none revealed the answer. Most didn't even include the word antimony.

I grabbed the dictionary. It defined antimony as "a silver metal." Somehow, even though it was obvious that silver metal could have been used to set stones, I knew the intended spiritual meaning was deeper. What was antimony? And what was it going to teach me?

Months passed, and I had almost given up

discovering the lesson hidden in antimony. But the verse kept coming back to my mind, time and again. I knew this must be an important brass nugget, but I was no closer to finding an answer to the puzzle.

∞

I DROVE SLOWLY along the hedge-lined lanes of the local countryside, the sun beating down through the windshield. Becoming drowsy, I decided to stop at the next little village for a cup of tea. As I slowed to find a parking space, I noticed a junk shop a few doors down from the café, the sign declaring "Antiques and Collectables." Hunger and thirst were forgotten.

A bell tinkled as I entered the shop's dim interior. The elderly proprietor looked up from his paper and peered at me over his spectacles, with only the lift of an eyebrow to acknowledge my presence. Walking up and down, scanning the clutter, I found nothing to tempt me. When I turned to go, I noticed a cardboard box of books under a low shelf beside the door.

On my knees, careless of my white blouse, I rummaged through the box. In the dusty jumble, I found a copy of H.V. Morton's *In the Steps of St. Paul*. Morton's books usually bring big prices, but this was an absolute steal. I paid for my treasure and went next door for a cup of tea, a slice of cake, and a peek inside my new bargain.

H.V. Morton was among the first travel writers. He wrote in the early 1900s for those who had never moved beyond their village. I already owned two of his books, *In the Footsteps of the Master* and *In Search of England*, so I knew I would enjoy this latest find.

I was delighted by Morton's vivid descriptions of the scenery and people he saw as he followed Paul's travels. But it wasn't until a few weeks later, when I was halfway through the book, that I discovered I had found more than a bargain that day; I had found the answer to "antimony." Morton described a Middle Eastern lady with black kohl eye makeup and added, "Since Old Testament times, kohl has been made from a plant called antimony."[4]

Aha! Antimony means blackness or darkness.

The Lord had taken great care to set my stones in darkness? Then I saw. Not knowing the purpose of my trials was like stumbling along in darkness. But the darkness was to *enhance their brilliance*.

How it could enhance their brilliance I did not know, but I dropped Morton open on the kitchen table and ran to get my notebook, where I recorded that thought as a prize brass nugget.

Months later, another old book built on this idea. It likened suffering to the dark velvet on which a diamond merchant displays his finest gems. I added that nugget to my notebook, and underneath it, in large letters, I wrote, "God has purposefully set my stones in the darkness of not understanding to enhance their brilliance."

Brass Nugget 9: No Offense

A few weeks later, the daily reading from another old devotional was, "Blessed is he, whosoever shall not be offended in Me" (Matthew 11:6 KJV).

Underneath was a poem:

> Blessed are you, O child of God, who
> suffers,
> And cannot understand,
> The reason for your pain, yet gladly
> leaves
> Your life in His blest Hand.
> Yes, blessed are you, whose faith is *not*
> *offended* [emphasis added]
> By trials unexplained, by mysteries
> unsolved, past understanding
> Until the goal is gained.[5]

I was "offended," for I could not understand why I was not healed. Prayer had brought no release from panic attacks and depression. My problem was not that I doubted God's ability to heal, but that *I knew He could.*

I had once been present in a small group when a dramatic healing took place. This was not a big meeting with all the fanfare, just a Thursday night Bible study with about a dozen close friends. I saw a friend's leg, which had been shortened by a car accident, grow more than an inch in a fraction of a second. After that night, he no longer needed his built-up shoe. In many ways it would have been easier for me had I not seen that healing, as the question underlying my struggle was, why has God not healed me?

Yet Matthew 11:6 asked that I be "not offended."

I had never heard it translated in that way before, so I checked other versions. The NIV translated it, "Blessed is the man who does not fall away on account of me." The Living Bible rendered it, "Blessed are those who don't doubt Me." To whom was Jesus speaking? Who was in danger of falling away? Who was it that doubted?

The minister of the church I now attended taught that to correctly understand a portion of scripture, it is important to ask questions. Who is speaking? Who is the intended audience? When and where was it spoken? What precedes it and what follows? The whole chapter must be read.

I discovered that *Blessed are those who don't doubt Me* was said in response to John the Baptist's question, "Are you *really* the one we are waiting for, or shall we keep on looking?" (Matthew 11:3 TLB) (emphasis added). It was John the Baptist who doubted!

How could he doubt that Jesus was the long-promised Messiah? It was he who cried out, "Look! There is the Lamb of God who takes away the world's sin!" in John 1:29 (TLB). He saw the Spirit descend on Jesus like a dove and heard the voice from heaven declare, "This is my Beloved Son and I am wonderfully pleased with Him" (Matthew 3:16 TLB). It was John who said of Jesus, "He shall baptize you with the Holy Spirit and with fire" (Matthew 3:11 TLB). How, then, could John doubt?

According to Matthew 11:2, by this time John was in prison. The loneliness of a dark cell caused the great man of God to doubt. Had John prayed for release? Had he expected Jesus would rescue him? Is that why Jesus sent word to him that *blessed is he who is not offended in Me?* How amazing; even John the Baptist had low times. That thought gave me comfort.

Brass Nugget 10: Stumbling Blocks or Stepping Stones

The Christian bookshop buzzed with activity. The sign across the window advertised "All Stock Reduced." Women crowded round a table of heavily discounted books. I waited for a break in the circumference of bodies and made my move.

The once-neat piles were now chaos. I picked up volume after volume, flicking through the pages or reading the blurb before consigning each back to the jumble. Then I found a small paperback, *The Wigglesworth Standard,* by Peter J. Madden. I had heard of Smith Wigglesworth and often thought I would like to know more about him. I decided to buy that one.

As I walked to the counter to pay, I read the back cover. "God confirmed Smith Wigglesworth's ministry, with powerful signs following. A few of these included the deaf hearing, cancers cured, legs and feet creatively formed where only stumps had existed previously, healing the violently insane, and fourteen being raised from the dead."[6]

As I stood in line, a sceptical thought raced through my mind. *Legs and feet formed out of thin air?* Why did I find it hard to believe that legs and feet could grow in an instant? I *saw* my friend's leg grow and *heard* the deep thud it made as it grew. "Why be sceptical?" I asked myself, "If the Lord can make a leg grow an inch or more, He can just as easily grow a whole new one." But I was by nature a sceptic. On the morning after I saw my friend's leg grow, I woke wondering if I had really seen it. I finally phoned John's home. His wife, Linda, answered. I asked tentatively, "Did what I think I saw last night really happen?

Linda had laughed. "Well, all I know is, I've a lot of trouser legs to let down."

My thoughts were interrupted by the cashier asking, "Can I help you?"

As I walked back to the car, I considered my sceptical reaction. I wondered about the nature of faith. People say, "I'll believe it when I see it." I had seen a miracle, yet still found it hard to believe in miracles. I pondered this all the way to the parking lot. I couldn't wait to get home to start reading this book.

The Wigglesworth Standard was not what I expected, for it focused, not so much on the miracles, but on Wigglesworth's deep prayer life and his constant search to know the Lord more intimately. Excerpts from his sermons were also included, and I found them inspiring.

Over the following weeks I read, underlined, and took notes. I had expected the great man of faith to have a life of blessing, but Smith Wigglesworth's life had a surprising side: he knew great suffering! When he was in his seventies, he endured the excruciating pain of kidney stones for six years. Though he prayed for healing, it didn't come. When he passed the stones, he lost so much blood that he became ashen grey and had to be wrapped in blankets to be kept warm. Yet he continued to preach, and God healed many people through him even while he remained in that weaken state.

No one could say that Wigglesworth lacked faith. He knew God could heal him, but though He did not, the man did not question. He accepted his suffering. Wigglesworth was *not offended*.

Instead, he preached: "There is no way into the deep things of God but by a broken spirit."[7]

He said, "It seems to me as if I have had a thousand road engines come over my life to break me up like a potter's vessel."[8]

Wigglesworth's acceptance of suffering touched me deeply. These next three Wigglesworth quotes, I wrote in my notebook as prized nuggets:

"The best thing that you ever could have is a great trial."[9]

"Great faith is the product of great fights, great testimonies are the outcome of great tests, and great triumphs can only come out of great trials."[10]

"Every stumbling block must become a stepping stone and every opposition must become an opportunity."[11]

And underneath, in large block letters, I wrote:

"My stones can be stumbling blocks or stepping stones. Lord, help me to step up."

Brass Nugget 11: If Only

I walked the half mile to the letter box, enjoying the bracing air. The dogs ran ahead of me, darting here and there after scent trails. I called them to heel as I reached the end of our lane so they wouldn't run out onto the busy road. They sat panting, tongues lolling, as I opened the letter box.

One small envelope lay in the bottom. Even before I turned it over to see the handwriting, the quality of the paper told me it was from Kaye. Most people sent text messages or emails, but Kaye wrote letters.

I opened it carefully, not wanting to tear the envelope. Along with an invitation to afternoon tea, Kaye had written, "In every life there is an 'If Only.' A tragedy, a heartbreak, that is unfathomable. Trust Jesus. Give Him your 'If Only.' Don't struggle, dear... you are loved."

Yet I did struggle, for my list of brass nuggets was becoming more confronting. I still had many unanswered questions that kept me awake at night.

AS I ENTERED Kaye's cottage, the warmth of the fire greeted me along with a tantalizing aroma of homemade scones hot from the oven. A white cloth covered the table in her tiny kitchen. We all served ourselves and returned to the sitting room to balance plates and teacups on our knees. I glanced from face to face, each so dear, and silently thanked the Lord for these precious women.

Dianna leaned over and passed me a paperback. "I found this in a garage sale. I just finished reading it." She flashed a smile, then continued in a more thoughtful tone. "I think you'll find it helpful."

Green Leaf in Drought by Isobel Kuhn is the account of missionaries trapped in inland China after the Communists closed the borders to all foreigners in 1951. Day by day, the husband and wife with their tiny daughter faced the prospect of death by starvation or freezing or at the hands of the communist overseers.

The husband had to present himself at the village office each morning. Many people who went to that office never came back. Every morning when he said good-bye to his wife, they knew it might be for the last time. They had prayed for release, yet release had not come. As the months dragged on, the family slipped into hopelessness.

Among their meagre possessions was a book by the great Bible teacher, Andrew Murray. Isobel spoke of a chapter in that book that told how to endure trials. Murray suggested applying Acts 27:27–29, "… as we were driven to and fro in the sea of Adria…they let go four anchors from the stern and prayed for the day." When driven about by the cruel winds of suffering, when caught in the storms that threaten to sweep away all that is dear, Murray[12] suggested letting down these "four anchors" by saying:

1. He brought me here. It is by His will I am in this straight place, and in that fact I will rest.
2. He will keep me here in His love and give me grace to behave as His child.
3. Then He will make the trial a blessing, teaching me the lessons He intends for me to learn.
4. In His good time He can bring me out again,

how and when He knows.

Murray abbreviated it like this:

1. I am here by God's appointment,
2. In His keeping,
3. Under His training,
4. For His time.

Cold, hungry, and ill, the missionaries knelt and told Jesus they accepted their suffering as from His hand and not from the hand of the enemy. Just as Paul had seen himself a prisoner of Christ, not of Rome, they would see themselves as His prisoners, not the Communists'.

The bravery of that little family humbled me.

I began to copy Andrew Murray's four points into my notebook, but stopped at Point 1 and could go no further: *He brought me here. It is by His will that I am in this straight place.*

Could I say that God brought me here, to this marriage with all its demands? No, I couldn't say that. It was my intense longing to be loved that made me ignore the scripture, "Do not be unequally yoked to an unbeliever." It was disobedience that had brought me here, and my old church had taught that suffering is punishment for disobedience.

Many nights I had lain awake with "if-onlys" going round and round in my head. I thought that if only I'd stayed in my little cottage, without all these pressures, maybe I would have recovered by now.

When discussing my regrets with Elizabeth one day, she said, "Don't you think God knew you would make that choice? Don't you think He can make all things work together for good because you love Him? Don't wonder about what you might have done. Just be the Lord's person right where you are."

They were comforting words, but they didn't keep regret from eating me up.

Brass Nugget 12: Redeeming Love

The familiar Old Testament stories are easy to read with the mind in neutral. But God was about to give me a jolt.

The daily reading was 2 Samuel 12:24–25:

> Then David comforted Bathsheba; and when he slept with her, she conceived and gave birth to a son and named him Solomon. And the Lord loved the baby and sent congratulations and blessings through Nathan the prophet. (TLB)

David committed adultery with Bathsheba, yet she was blessed to give birth to Solomon. And the Lord loved the baby and sent congratulations and blessings! Yes, I know, David and Bathsheba's first son died. But of all David's wives, it was Bathsheba who was honoured by God to be the mother of the builder of the temple.

Slowly it dawned on me. Jesus' love is a redeeming love. David's sin did not stop God from bringing about His purposes. Therefore, in spite of anything I had done, God could still use me for His purposes. On my knees, I confessed once again my sin of marrying a man whom I knew was not a committed Christian, but this time I was able to accept the full and completed forgiveness my Lord had died to win for me. Tears of release came, and with them came a determination that my marriage would bring about the Lord's purposes.

IMPORTANT NOTE: Please do not misunderstand; "accepting our stones" does not mean you should learn to tolerate abuse. If you are caught in the grip of a demeaning or violent relationship, be assured that God does not want you to meekly accept the situation. Please read the Footnote beginning on page 209 before going any further. Your life may depend upon it.

∞

Chapter 9

∞

A Giant Leap

LITTLE BRASS NUGGETS came from many sources: Bible study, sermons, old books, and one from a magnet on a friend's fridge. Nugget by nugget Jesus led me, inching me closer and closer to the edge of a big step.

A step I did not want to take. The step of unequivocal acceptance of my stones, with no strings attached.

This acceptance was not a formula. It wasn't a bargain with God, that I would do this for Him if He gave me what I wanted. It was as naked as Job's declaration, "Though He slay me yet will I trust Him" (Job 13:15 KJV).

Oh, how terrifying was the very sight of that step! Yet each succeeding brass nugget produced more evidence, overwhelming evidence, until I knew I had to take it.

Brass Nugget 13: Shaken Awake

The old stone church where I worshipped was freezing in winter. Early each Sunday, while the frost lay thick on the ground and the congregation slept warm in their beds, an elderly deacon arrived to do battle with the antiquated heating system. His dedication to this chore was nothing less than heroic, but unfortunately, his efforts usually only yielded their full effect just as the sermon began.

Such was the case one Sunday morning. Though the pews were hard, the heat made me sleepy, and I found myself nodding. My chin hit my chest. Our minister's voice broke into my semi-consciousness as he said, "Reading from Second Corinthians 11:24 to 27, Paul wrote:

> Five times I received from the Jews the
> forty lashes minus one. Three times I
> was beaten with rods, once I was
> pelted with stones, three times I was
> shipwrecked, I spent a night and a day
> in the open sea, I have been constantly
> on the move. I have been in danger
> from rivers, in danger from bandits, in
> danger from my fellow Jews, in danger
> from Gentiles; in danger in the city, in
> danger in the country, in danger at sea;
> and in danger from false believers. I
> have labored and toiled and have often
> gone without sleep; I have known
> hunger and thirst and have often gone

without food; I have been cold and
naked." (NIV)

I was wide awake now, hearing this portion of
the scripture as if for the first time. My mind, fed
by years of prosperity teaching, had skimmed over
this passage, or shut it out, choosing instead to
focus on the miracles Paul performed. This time,
that list of sufferings broke through. I saw the
reality, the cruel beatings, the stoning, the
shipwrecks, and years in a Roman prison. Paul's life
was not one of endless miracles. He suffered. How
could I be so blind?

As soon as I arrived home, I opened my Bible
to read 2 Corinthians 11:24-27.

It is easy to read quickly, letting the words slip
through the mind, conveying facts but not stirring
the emotions. This time, I read slowly to let myself
imagine each hardship as though it were happening
to me.

After years of suffering and pain, Paul stated
without reservation in Romans 8:28, that all things
work together for good for those who love God.
Would I ever be able to say that?

Over the months that followed, each time I
found a comment of Paul's on suffering, I wrote it
on a page set aside for that purpose. These three
were especially meaningful to me:

"…we also glory in our sufferings, because we know that suffering produces perseverance" (Romans 5:3 NIV).

"For our light and momentary troubles are achieving for us an eternal glory that far outweighs them all" (2 Corinthians 4:17 NIV).

"Do not be surprised at the painful trial you are suffering, as though something strange were happening to you" (1 Peter 4:12 NIV).

As I turned back through my notebook each day, I often stopped at, "Blessed is he who is not offended in Me." I was still offended. I still questioned. But pinpricks of light glittered though the blackness.

On the page of Paul's quotes, I wrote in large letters, "The thorn in the side remained, yet Paul was not offended." The Lord's word, "My grace is sufficient for you, for my power is made perfect in weakness" (2 Corinthians 12:9 NIV), was a good enough answer for Paul.

The Living Bible rendered that verse, "My power shows up best in weak people." Could it be that my prolonged suffering would show the Lord's power? I added that thought to my list.

With pen in hand, I considered the comfort Paul's letters gave to believers and the comfort they had given me. A new thought took me by surprise. Those letters may not have been written if Paul had not spent so much time in prison. Paul suffered that we might know the comfort of his words!

Down through the centuries… words from Paul's pen came to me, "Now I rejoice in what I am suffering for you" (Colossians 1:2 NIV).

Brass Nugget 14: Given No Help?

Much of a mother's life is spent waiting. Waiting for the children to come out of school, sitting in the car outside music lessons, sport practices, or the dentist. My busy life gave me little time to read, but I formed the habit of always carrying an old Christian book in my handbag so I could make good use of the time I spent waiting. Even in checkout lines in the supermarket, instead of browsing through magazines, I would pull out a book and read. I am astounded at the number of books I have read in those snippets of time.

Kaye had given me a book by the famous missionary to India, Amy Carmichael, *His Thoughts Said…His Father Said*. This little book is ideal for such occasions, as it can be opened and read from any page.

I sat outside my sons' school one afternoon reading it when I came to: "His thoughts said, 'The fight is fierce.' His Father said, 'He who is near to his Captain is sure to be a target for the archers.'"[13]

It was a lovely thought, but I did not feel close to my Captain. I felt like a straggler in the ranks. I often asked myself, "Why is it that some Christians have pleasant lives full of blessings while others have long years of pain and suffering?"

Was it possible that the blessed ones walked so closely with the Lord that they were under the covering of His protection? What did that say of me? Was I attacked because I was far from the Lord? My old church had taught that very thing, and though I was beginning to see things differently, guilt still twisted inside me. Sitting in the car, I absentmindedly flicked through the pages and this heading caught my eye, A Son of Kohath.[14] As I read, Amy Carmichael opened up a new way of looking at lack of blessings. She noted that, according to Numbers 7:6-8, Moses gave carts and oxen to the Levites and Gershonites and Meronites but he gave *nothing* to the Kohathites, because they were to carry on their shoulders the holy things, for which they were responsible.

All the other priestly tribes had help in their task of carrying the curtains and poles of the tabernacle. They were given oxen to pull carts, allowing them to ride through the wilderness with no effort. But the Kohathites had nothing to help them carry their load. Did they look at the others' carts with envy, asking why they were given no help? Or did they feel humbled by the honour, given them from the very presence of God, to personally bear the weight of the golden treasure from the Holy of Holies?

Was I given no relief from the burden I carried

because it was a holy duty?

Could this suffering bring true spiritual treasure, pure gold instead of brass?

This nugget seemed to expand "honour and privilege" into realms I could only glimpse.

Chapter 10

Blameless

Brass Nugget 15: A Spiritual Inheritance

A.W. TOZER'S *The Pursuit of God* fitted neatly in my handbag. Though small in size, it is immense in spiritual content. I found it impossible to read more than a few sentences at a time, for it is a book that arrests the spirit. Time and time again I had to close my eyes and let a thought sink in.

I was still absorbing the concept that those who seem to be given few blessings are entrusted instead with spiritual treasure, when Tozer brought it into sharp focus. He wrote:

> When the Lord divided Canaan among the tribes of Israel, Levi received no share of the land. God said to him simply, 'I am thy part and thine inheritance, and by those words made him richer than all his brethren, richer

than all the kings and rajas who have ever lived in the world. And there is a spiritual principle here, a principle still valid for every priest of the Most High God. The man who has God for his treasure has all things in One. Many ordinary treasures may be denied him, or if he is allowed to have them, the enjoyment of them will be so tempered that they will never be necessary to his happiness. Or if he must see them go, one after one, he will scarcely feel a sense of loss, for having the Source of all things he has in One all satisfaction, all pleasure, all delight. Whatever he may lose he has actually lost nothing, for he now has it all in One, and he has it purely, legitimately and forever.[15]

If a Levite had been in my previous church, he would have been told to "claim your inheritance." The leaders would have advised, "God does not want you to go without. Pray through to victory!"

Levi's tribe received no material inheritance, but was set apart for deep intimacy with God. I added this to my list of nuggets beneath my entry about the Kohathites.

Brass Nugget 16: God's Time, God's Place

My Bible lay open before me, but I was too weary to concentrate. I closed my eyes and prayed,

Lord, I am tired of being tired, and reached for the old devotional.

"Sorrow is better than laughter; for by the sadness of the countenance the heart is made better" (Ecclesiastes 7:3, NIV). The devotional went on to say:

> God never uses anybody to a large degree until after he breaks that one all to pieces. Joseph had more sorrow than all the other sons of Jacob, and it led him out into a ministry of bread for all nations.[16]

Broken to pieces!

Why must we be broken to be of service? Everything within me rebelled against this. Then, as I sat writhing, resistant, there came a gentle whisper, "Man of Sorrows, acquainted with grief."[*] And then, like the last notes of a haunting melody, "Jesus broken for me,"[**] flowed through my heart, stilling the turmoil. Quiet filtered into the deep places and, amazed at the stillness, I remembered the words of Smith Wigglesworth: "There is no way into the deep things of God but by a broken spirit."

The next morning, I turned to Genesis to read again the story of Joseph.

Joseph's brothers had been the cause of his suffering; yet in Genesis 45:5, Joseph says to them,

---

[*] Isaiah 53:3 (KJV)
[**] I Corinthians 11:24

"Come closer to me. Don't feel badly, don't blame yourselves for selling me. God was behind it. He sent me here ahead of you to save lives. So you see? It wasn't you who sent me here, but God" (author's paraphrase).

Joseph did not blame his brothers. He accepted his suffering as from the hand of God. Did he always see it this way, or did this understanding come after he had been made ruler of Egypt? Maybe the revelation of God's loving forethought came only as his brothers stood before him.

Thrown into a pit, sold as a slave, wrongfully accused, falsely imprisoned and forgotten, year after year of suffering. If Joseph had been in my former church, he would be accused of being out of the will of God. I laughed aloud at the thought, for God had Joseph in the centre of His will, in just the right place—albeit a most uncomfortable place— for a very long time.

I wrote in my notebook: "Though years pass and nothing seems to change, God has a long-term plan."

Brass Nugget 17: Blameless

My list of nuggets was now pages long; my notebook challenged me with scripture after scripture that revealed the errors of what I'd previously been taught. But my mind was ensnared, and the error so imbedded that the false beliefs were not easy to shed. My moments of profound peace were fleeting, and most days I struggled.

My previous church preached that suffering came only to those who were in sin. They said Job suffered because he feared the future, which showed lack of faith. As a proof text, they quoted, "What I feared has come upon me. What I dreaded has happened to me" (Job 3:25 NIV). The idea that Job had brought suffering upon himself by sin was firmly entrenched in my thinking. The book of Job always made me feel very guilty, and I didn't like to read it.

But one morning, half asleep, I turned to Job and read through the opening verses. I had heard it all before, but I kept reading, not really paying attention, until verse 8 snapped me awake.

"Then the Lord said to Satan, 'Have you considered My servant Job? There is no one on earth like him; he is blameless and upright'" (Job 1:8 NIV).

Blameless! The Lord said Job was *blameless.* Not only that, but "there is no one like him on all the earth." Job was the most holy man of his day! Why had I not seen this before? How did my church get it so wrong?

But instead of bringing me comfort, this new revelation awakened more questions. Why had God allowed Satan to strip the blameless Job of everything?

Why is it necessary to suffer to come close to

God? Why must my stones be set in darkness? How can pain be strengthening? I did not understand, but I opened my notebook and wrote, "Suffering comes even to those whose lives are blameless."

Those words stood stark on a new page. I did not like to look at them. This was too much to take in. I shut my notebook and walked away. How could I get my head around the concept that Satan asked to bring suffering to blameless Job—and God gave him permission?

Brass Nugget 18: Permission Is Given

A large wooden cross stood at the front of the church. The worshipers were unusually quiet; Good Friday services have that effect. Though I could almost quote the familiar scripture readings word for word, one verse echoed in my heart:

"Simon, Simon, Satan has asked to sift all of you as wheat" (Luke 22:31 NIV).

There it was again. Satan had to ask permission.

I drove home from church in turmoil. *Satan had to ask.*

Satan could not touch Peter until permission was given. And, though I struggled to comprehend it, God gave His permission. Peter was sifted as wheat, and not just through his denial of Jesus. At the end of his life, Peter's hands were tied, and he was led away to be crucified.

Brass Nugget 19: The Way of Heroes

I often stopped to browse at the table of discounted books outside the Christian bookstore. On a number of occasions, I noticed *Foxe's Book of Martyrs*. Once I even picked it up. I did not want to buy that book—nothing about the cover or the title appealed to me. It was as if I knew that this book would be confronting.

A few weeks later, we met at Kaye's for afternoon tea. Above the chatter I heard someone mention *that book*, and my ears pricked up. "Last century, most homes had a *Foxe's Book of Martyrs* beside their Bible." I needed to purchase *that book*, and I needed to do it before the store closed. I finished my cup of tea and made hurried goodbyes, explaining, "I'm off to the bookstore," leaving my friends somewhat startled at my sudden exit.

It was only a short drive to the local Christian bookstore, and for once I found parking not far from the door. I made the precious purchase and hurried back to the car, where I didn't wait, but took the book from the paper bag and began reading immediately.

I was humbled.

Stephen, stoned.

Paul, beheaded.

Philip, crucified.

Matthew, beheaded.

Barnabas, burnt to death.

James the Lesser, clubbed to death.

Mark, dragged to death.

Andrew, crucified.

Thomas, speared to death.

Luke, hanged.

Peter, crucified.

John, exiled to a lonely island.

These were Jesus' own—and they were not spared.

The list of martyrs went on and on, down through the centuries, one faithful believer after another joyful to be called to share in Christ's sufferings.

On the last night of the year, while others celebrated, I read late into the night. Page after page confronted me with the suffering of those whose lives were *blameless*. I had nowhere to go intellectually, for if what my church had taught was correct, then all those amazing Christians who had been tormented and died for Jesus must have been in sin. Otherwise, God would have performed a miraculous last-minute rescue for each one.

I could see that was ridiculous. But I did not want to accept that God allowed suffering. If He did, I couldn't pray my pain away. I would just have to tough it out.

But, in light of the mounting evidence, it was illogical to hold onto prosperity teaching any longer. How I could expect my life to be heaven on earth while others who followed Jesus suffered torture and death? Did I really expect to live a cushy, satin-lined life, protected from difficulty? Is that what a follower of Jesus should expect? Reluctantly, I came to the conclusion that history— and the scriptures—show the opposite.

I wrote three full pages in my journal that night. The conclusions I had come to through *Foxe's Book of Martyrs* could not be unfolded in a few sentences.

∞

Chapter 11

∞

Challenged, Confronted, Perplexed

I FELT UNSETTLED through the first months of my second year of collecting nuggets. All the bits of truth I was uncovering pushed me to a conclusion I did not want to make. Sometimes when I read through my notes, my struggle to make sense of it caused inner anguish. Other days, as I sat reading or praying, the Holy Spirit's presence enfolded and comforted me.

Three times in less than a week, from three different sources, I heard Oswald Chambers' *My Utmost for His Highest* quoted. Being now more sensitive to the Lord's promptings, I drove to town to buy a copy. I glanced at my watch as I left the bookstore. There was time to see Elizabeth for a chat and a cup of tea before I collected my boys from school.

All who met Elizabeth were captivated by her charm. Tall, elegant, gracious, and with impeccable taste, she spoke at many Christian women's groups and was involved in much charity work. Her schedule would have exhausted a woman half her age, and yet she remained serene and ever ready to open her home and her arms to all. Elizabeth bore the title of Lady, but she was more than earthly nobility; she was truly a daughter of the King of Kings, a Princess Warrior.

I drove up her drive, sweeping between the neat box hedges, topiary, and white standard roses. After parking, I exited the car, unbuckled my daughter and lifted her from her car seat, then climbed the front steps and rang Elizabeth's doorbell. Balancing my little girl on my hip, I gazed at the peaceful beauty of the garden as I waited.

The door flew open, and Elizabeth welcomed me with a smile and a hug. "What a lovely surprise. I am glad you came, as I have a little gift for you."

I followed her down the hall, past lovely rooms where antique furniture gleamed and chintz curtains swept the floor in heavy folds. In the kitchen, a battered copy of *My Utmost for His Highest* lay on the table.

Elizabeth turned to me. "I feel very strongly that the Lord wants you to have my copy of…" But before she could finish, I told her I had just bought one. We jumped up and down and hugged each other at the Lord's confirmation.

So began a new phase in my journey.

I tried to absorb the daily reading from *My Utmost for His Highest* at night, but it was not easy.

Chambers' concepts are lofty, and his words at times are confronting, even harsh. Every page challenged me. I needed a fresh mind to face the truths Chambers revealed.

So I established a new routine: I read the old devotional at night and *My Utmost* in the morning. With my notebook and Bible close by, I ploughed on. At first I struggled to understand, but as the weeks passed, I found the daily readings were just the mental and spiritual exercise I needed. I couldn't bear to miss a day.

Four extremely challenging statements brought me to a crisis point. The first of these:

> In the history of the Christian Church the tendency has been to evade being identified with the sufferings of Jesus Christ; men have sought to procure the carrying out of God's order by a shortcut of our own. God's way is always the way of suffering, the way of the long, long trial.[17]

My previous church certainly did not want to be identified with the sufferings of Jesus. They demanded miracles, victory, blessings, and prosperity, and they wanted them now!

I'd since learned that was not God's way. But surely, I thought, ours must not *always* be the way of suffering, not *always* the path through a long, long trial! Surely not. For doesn't the 23rd Psalm say, "He makes me to lie down in green pastures; He leads me by the still waters" (Psalm 23:2 NKJV)?

But then, I remembered it also says, "...though I walk through the valley of the shadow of death..." (Psalm 23:4 NKJV).

And Isaiah said:

> When you pass through the waters, I will
>   be with you;
> And through the rivers, they shall not
>   overflow you.
> When you walk through the fire, you
>   shall not be burned,
> Nor shall the flame scorch you. (Isaiah
> 43:2 NKJV)

The promise of protection is *when* suffering comes, not *if*.

Jesus said, "In the world you *will* have tribulation" (John 16:33 NKJV). Though he added, "but be of good cheer, I have overcome the world," that does not wipe away the *You will have tribulation.* I considered the possibility that the long trial could be part of the plan for everyone.

A few days later, I read "If anyone desires to come after Me, let him deny himself, and take up his cross, and follow Me" (Matthew 16:24 NKJV).

Take up *his* cross leapt from the page. Every follower will have a personal cross, a painful difficulty that they must carry. Jesus knew it is never easy to follow Him. How had I never seen that before?

I pondered whether those who seemed to not suffer were merely hiding their suffering, or refusing to "take up their cross," finding instead a shortcut around it.

A second Oswald Chambers quote took my thinking further:

> Why shouldn't we go through heartbreaks? Through these doorways God is opening up ways of fellowship with His Son…He comes with the grip of the pierced hand of His Son and says, "Enter into fellowship with Me. Arise and shine… If through a broken heart God can bring His purposes to pass in the world then thank Him for breaking your heart.[18]

This was too hard. Too hard! How I could ever thank God for breaking my heart?

The third quote seemed to answer my cry:

> When I stop telling God what I want, He can catch me up for what He wants without hindrance.[19]

What? I had spent my whole Christian life telling God what I wanted. This was all too new and different. I had never heard anything like it.

A fourth and last quote made me face the stark reality of 2 Timothy 4:6, "I am ready to be poured out like a drink offering" (NKJV).

Chambers wrote:

> Externally life may be the same; the
> difference is in the will...
> Tell God you are ready to be offered and
> God will prove Himself to be all you ever
> dreamed He would be.[20]

Externally, life may be the same; the difference is in the will.

Tell God you are ready to be offered.

I now knew what needed to be done. I must truly accept my stones and hills. To accept that externally, life may be the same; there may be no glorious outcome. I must choose to be God's person even if nothing changed.

Everything within me screamed, "No, not that, surely there is another way!"

"I'll fast, I'll pray. I don't want things to be the same."

"I want this horrible depression to leave me."

"I want the fear and panic attacks to stop.

"I want my husband to understand me."

"I want all the visitors to stop coming."

"I want deliverance!"

I panicked at the realization of the direction the Lord was leading me. As Andrew Murray had explained it, I must say with my whole being:

1. He brought me here. It is by His will I am in this straight place, and in that fact I will rest.

2. He will keep me here in His love and give me

grace to behave as His child.

3. Then He will make the trial a blessing, teaching me the lessons He intends for me to learn.

4. In His good time He can bring me out again, how and when He knows.

I could see that step before me, but I could not take it. I could not say those four things.

It was the fourth point that gave me the most trouble. I did not like what it suggested. "In His good time He *can* bring me out." *Can.* Not w*ill.* That was a frightening concept. I needed a miracle and couldn't bear the thought that one might never come.

Days and nights were filled with reasoning, struggling, praying, looking for another way out. To live out the truth of "iron from stones" was too hard… just too hard.

I looked back through my notebook, trying to draw strength from the little pieces of brass I had collected, but they seemed to have tarnished. "Externally life may be the same; the difference is in the will" had taken all the shine from them.

In this crisis of will, I had no one to help me. This was too personal, too deep to tell even Kaye. Weeks passed and then months as I hovered, balanced on the edge of a precipice, about to fall back into the depths.

Brass Nugget 20: A Strong Wall of Facts

In addition to our regular afternoon teas, Dianna, Helen, and Kathryn began to meet weekly at my home. We had no leader and no set study in these informal get-togethers. We would come with our Bibles, old books, and journals and share what the Lord had been showing us through the week, along with sandwiches, tears, and triumphs. But I couldn't talk about my struggles. I just couldn't find the words.

Gentleness surrounded Dianna like a beautiful garment. She spoke rarely, but when she did, her words were precious. There was such grace and humility about her that I felt shallow in her presence, yet she lifted me up to see Jesus as she saw Him, with childlike trust. When excited, her trusting eyes sparkled and she seemed to glow.

It was in this state that she sat waiting for her turn to share. I knew it was going to be special, so I waited expectantly. She opened her notebook and read something she had written.

> There is a high wall, strongly built, that separates Hope from Despair. Standing on that wall are three figures, Feeling, Faith, and Fact. They stand firmly, holding hands and looking to Jesus. Strong winds of circumstance sweep across that wall. These three must be on their guard to remain balanced, facing Jesus on the side of Hope. Sometimes the

winds of circumstance blow so strongly
that Feeling, the weakest of the three,
falls to the side of Despair, tumbling
through the nothingness. Faith, quick and
sure, reaches out to catch Feeling, but in
doing so loses the grip of Fact. Now
Feeling and Faith are falling fast.

Fact—strong, secure, immovable upon
that wall of God's existence, His
provable reality—takes hold of Faith and
pulls Faith up. Then Faith pulls up
Feeling, once again to stand firm upon
the wall, facing Hope.

I said nothing to my friends of what that meant
to me. But after they left, I sat thinking:

*I see it now. My feelings pull Faith down into despair;
only Fact is solid and immovable. That makes sense. So what
do I know as fact?*

The Lord is all-powerful.

The Lord loves me.

The Lord answers prayer.

As I looked at those three facts, an absolute
certainty grew within me. The Lord *is* all-powerful—
and He has the final say! The Lord *does* love me. He
proved it by sending Jesus to die in my place. He *does*
answer prayer. Therefore, as my circumstances have
not changed after much prayer, they must be for my
ultimate benefit.

The long struggle was finally over.

I prayed, "All right, Lord, I accept that You have

brought me to this hard place. Even if depression and panic attacks are all my life will ever be, You can have Your Way, though I have no idea what You are doing or why."

To say a thing is relatively easy; to act on it is a different matter. Though I had prayed that prayer of acceptance, I was still blown about by every wind of circumstance, one moment sensing the Lord's presence and the next moment in the black well again, feeling alone and frightened as I looked for another way out. Though I desperately searched, I came back time and time again to the knowledge that there was no other way out. Though I had said I would accept my stones and hills, God had to teach me how to stand firm in the midst of them.

I began praying, "For I am poor and needy and my heart is wounded within me" (Psalm 109:22 NIV).

"Grant me a willing spirit to sustain me" (Psalm 51:12 NIV).

Nuggets could be found anywhere, at any time. I learned never to trust my memory, so if I found a nugget but didn't have my notebook, I would write on odd scraps, like the backs of envelopes or receipts, even on paper serviettes.

Three precious nuggets had languished, long forgotten, in the bottom of a little-used handbag stored with the rest on a shelf in my walk-in wardrobe. Wanting a lime green bag that had made its way to the very back, I stood on a chair to reach it. As I pulled it forward, three others tumbled down, spilling their contents all over the floor. I gathered up the mess of tissues, hair clips, used theatre tickets, and old lipsticks. As I dropped each item of rubbish into the wastebasket, I spied my handwriting on the back of a small envelope. I had written:

- Take hold of the black disappointment, break it open and extract some jewel of grace.
- An unaccepted sorrow only festers in the soul and drives us away from God rather than towards him.
- The sorrows in life cause us to rise towards God.

I had no idea when or where I had found those nuggets, but they spoke to my heart afresh.

My unaccepted sorrow had been festering in my soul for long enough. I wanted to rise toward God, so I told Him again and again that I did not regret His sending sorrow into my life and I was willing to accept it. But I did not know how to live each day in light of that.

Weeks passed. There were days when the words of the Lord were more than just theory; they were life, and the sun shone. But other days, I felt unable to move forward, every step was heavy, and if the sun shone, I didn't see it. Why did I swing so wildly? Why couldn't I keep moving steadily forward, or at least hold my ground?

My dear friends Kaye, Dianna, and Julia accepted my bad days. But some other friends, and some family members, were impatient with me. "Come on,

Edith, isn't it time you moved on?" "Just stop dwelling on the past." "Are you taking your medication, dear?" And then there were the people who didn't say a word, but they didn't need to; their faces spoke their thoughts.

I was already ashamed of myself, and the well-meaning words and impatient looks made me feel much worse. Few understood Post Traumatic Stress Disorder. I didn't understand it myself. The symptoms of PTSD would appear without warning, creeping upon me like a slow fog that could last for weeks.

On a Friday morning during one such episode, James strode through the kitchen, his arms loaded with files, and said hurriedly, "We will be coming straight from court so should be back here by 7 p.m." The door shut, then opened again, and James' worried face peered in. "You have remembered this evening's dinner guests?"

I looked at him blankly. I had forgotten.

I needed to organize myself, and quickly. I checked the fridge, made a list of what I needed, grabbed my handbag, and headed to the car. But the keys were not in my handbag. I ran back inside and searched through other bags, pockets, in every conceivable spot. Eventually, I found them in the fridge.

Flustered, and now very late, I drove to the city and then raced around the supermarket, throwing items into the trolley like a crazy lady. Even when I was finished there, my errands were not ended, for the French cheese James loved and expected to be served at every dinner party was only available at a delicatessen in the heart of the city.

I found a parking spot not far from the deli and dashed first to the florist and then into the store. My hands were full as I returned to the car with flowers, the balsa wood box containing the precious brie, and a cellophane box of chocolate truffles. I placed these items on the passenger seat, buckled up, and turned the ignition key. Only then did I see the parking ticket on the windshield. I had neglected to put money in the meter!

It was 2:30 p.m. when I finally arrived home. I left the groceries on the table and made a cup of tea. As I took the first sip, I remembered that the meat I'd intended to take out before I left for the city was still in the freezer.

My mind spun. Now I needed to rethink everything.

Late that evening, after the guests had left and James retreated to his study, I stumbled to the ironing room and slumped into my chair. How I longed to be organized, to think clearly, to be consistent. I prayed, "Lord, only last week I felt strong and confident. Now I feel hopeless. Last week, I was certain of your promises. Now, I'm full of fear that I'll never recover."

Brass Nugget 21: Wavering

I opened the Bible. The daily reading was Lamentations chapter three. I read through until I came to verses 55 and 56:

> I called on your name, O LORD,
>   from the depths of the pit.
> You heard my plea: "Do not close your
>   ears to my cry for relief." (NIV)

Jeremiah acknowledged that God heard his plea…then immediately, just the opposite… Do not close your ears? I marvelled that thousands of years before, the writer of Lamentations had experienced the wild swing between knowing the Lord's nearness and the feeling of abandonment.

I wrote those verses in my ring binder and underneath, I added: "Swinging emotions are normal. Accept the swings. Be grateful for the good times and remember them during the bad times."

∽

Chapter 12

∽

A New Name

ON THE THIRD New Year's Day since "Stones are Iron" had made such an impact, I looked back through my notes. As I turned the pages, a step-by-step pathway seemed to unfold before me. I had not come far along that path, for I was still a frail, frightened mess, coping by sheer willpower. But I longed to be normal, to function like other people.

Our little girl, now four, started school. Meeting all the new parents and interacting with the teacher was frightening. I kept smiling, but was sure everyone knew I was not "quite right." Kaye and the girls surrounded me with love and practical support. Kaye would write to me the most loving letters of encouragement. I prayed to be shown how I was to move on.

About the middle of that year, I walked along the

path that leads around the side of my church. I was running late, and the service had already started. I heard the congregation sing words I had learned long ago.

> I will change your name
> You shall no longer be called
> Wounded, outcast, lonely or afraid.
> I will change your name
> Your new name shall be
> Confidence, joyfulness, overcoming one
> Faithfulness, friend of God
> One who seeks My face. [21]

The words washed over me and held me motionless by the beauty, not only of the words, but also the music. Tears flowed, silently falling, cleansing.

Months later, I mentioned to the music director how the song had touched me and asked if we could sing it again soon. She looked puzzled and assured me she did not know the song and we had never sung it. I pressed her and said maybe she had been away and someone else had led the worship that day. But she said no, it would have been impossible, as she knew all the modern songs the church had copyright license to use, and that song was not among them. I felt shaken. I thought on top of everything else I was losing my mind.

I had been singing the song over and over for all these months, feeling the strength of the promise that the Lord would change my name from all those painful things to all the things I longed to be.

Now, the enemy whispered his lies, making me wonder if all the insights I had received from the Lord were merely self-deception. I was scared. Was I delusional?

I shared my fears with Kaye and the others, and they encouraged me not to worry. I should consider this memory-that-was–not-a-memory as a dream from the Lord. As unbelievable as it seemed, the only explanation was that I had dreamt it and slowly, over time, the dream had become like a memory.

The beauty of the words and the wonderful feeling of release and hope and peace had been so vivid. The song had become part of my life. Its promise was precious to me. The Lord would change my name!

In the Scriptures, name changes came with a change of the person's inner life. I was drawn in particular to Jacob's name change to Israel: from "usurper" to "he who wrestles with God." It became a theme that filled many pages of the ring binder that now replaced my battered notebook.

SLEEP EVADED ME. Thoughts of the strange dream and the song filled my mind. My face felt cold, so I snuggled down and pulled the blankets around my head. Through the tiny gap where the window curtains hadn't quite closed, a star shone. No sound broke the silence of our valley, held deep in the fold of three hills. The song's haunting melody drifted through my mind. The distant star's icy light flicked as I floated into sleep, my mind full of the promise of a new name, a new nature.

Brass Nugget 22: I Will Change Your Name

At three a.m., I woke with a start, instantly knowing I had to confess my name to God.

Confess my name to God? What did that even mean?

Heavy with sleep, I crept out of bed so as not to wake James, wrapped myself in a bulky quilt, and tiptoed downstairs along the dim passages to the ironing room.

Moonlight spilled in. The garden, silvered by frost, lay sleeping. I sat bundled in the quilt with my ring binder open on my knees. I knew I had to do something, but what, I didn't know.

I prayed and waited… the minutes passed… but nothing came to me. Finally, I drew a line down the middle of a page and on the left-hand side I wrote,

Wounded

Outcast

Lonely

Afraid

I stared at the blank space on the other side of the page for some time. Gradually, there came a deep knowing that Jesus was asking me to write my true name in the right column. But I didn't know what to write. Then Jesus spoke lovingly into my heart.

"Look carefully at these names. You have been wounded, you have been made an outcast, you have been made lonely, and you have been caused to be afraid. None of these things did you bring upon yourself, and there is no sin in them. They were done to you; you had no control over them. But let Me show you what you *do* have control over, and what you can confess to Me as your name."

From each name I drew an arrow, and then Jesus tenderly showed me what to write. He revealed to me all that had grown from those painful names.

Out of WOUNDED came a hardness of heart, the scar tissue of unforgiveness.

From OUTCAST came rejection. As I had been rejected, I was afraid to trust people for fear they would hurt me again, so unconsciously I rejected them.

From LONELY came self-pity and self-imposed isolation. Because I did not trust others, I did not reach out to them; I was shut away inside myself.

From AFRAID came fear itself.

Fear! How could fear be something that I needed to confess? Yet gently, Jesus showed me that fear is sin, because it is the opposite of faith. Fear is faithlessness.

How could I control my fear? It was so much a part of my life as to be inseparable from who I was. But, as an act of obedience, I confessed fear and every name that had grown out of the things that had been done to me, and I asked the Lord to change my name.

A very long time passed as I sat with pen in hand. It was now the early hours of the morning, and I was cold. But I did not move, trying to take it all in.

Over the years I had prayed to forgive, and I had willed myself to forgive. I had prayed blessings on those who had hurt me, and I had prayed that the things others had done to me would not be held against them. I honestly believed that I had forgiven, totally, unequivocally, unreservedly, for I knew that my own forgiveness was dependent upon it.

"But if you do not forgive others their sins, your Father will not forgive your sins" (Matthew 6:15 NIV).

"For in the same way you judge others, you will be judged, and with the measure you use, it will be measured to you" (Matthew 7:2 NIV).

Not only had I willed to forgive, but I was by nature a gentle, forgiving person.

The revelation that I still hid unforgiveness in my heart took me by surprise, but it was true. My kindness and gentleness were just on the surface, a veneer atop my true nature. It was this inner nature that the Lord longed for me to give over to Him.

Yes, I could see it all so clearly. Fear, unforgiveness, and self-pity had become firmly entrenched in my heart—they were my identity. But until this night, I had been unaware of their destructive presence.

I had seen the stones in my life as the enemy. Now, Jesus showed me that the enemies were within, and the battlefield was my own heart.

All the times I'd prayed for my circumstances to be changed, it was not the circumstances I should have been praying about, but my reaction to them.

Those in my former church might have said, "Ah! See? You did have secret sin! You were in bondage, and that is why you were depressed. If you just confessed and took authority over the spirits of unforgiveness and depression in Jesus' name, you would be free."

But I *had* confessed. I had "broken and bound," fasted, and prayed earnestly and persistently. But still the panic attacks, confusion, and depression remained.

To say that I was not set free because of sin is the core error of prosperity teaching. To follow that line of thought to its logical conclusion is to say that no one can be set free, for "all have sinned" (Rom. 3:23 NIV).

The next time the girls were together for our study, I showed them the page with the list of names. Dianna nodded in understanding, "Oh, that is just like the name exchanges in *Hinds' Feet on High Places* and *Mountains of Spices*. Kaye's got copies of both those books. Why don't you borrow them?"

Years ago I had read Hanna Hurnard's beautiful allegory, *Hinds' Feet on High Places*. I thought it lovely but had not understood much of it. Now, as I walked the paths of suffering myself, it touched me deeply. The similarities of that story to my own affected me profoundly. Scriptures that sang in my own heart were there in those books, and reading them in this new setting intensified their meaning until they felt like a fire within. Could it be that He who is the same yesterday, today, and forever leads all His dear ones along similar paths?

In that book, the character Much Afraid attained the High Places with the help of two travelling companions, Sorrow and Suffering. The Lord Himself had chosen them, yet Much Afraid could not bear to even look at them. As she journeyed, she learned to accept her two unattractive companions. The dark-clad pair led her through deserts, into shadowy valleys and up sheer precipices until they brought her to a lonely cave to confront her fears while a ferocious storm shook the mountain. She lay upon a stone altar and accepted.

I had been to the mountain cave where the storm of my doubts and fears raged. I, like Much Afraid, almost gave up everything the Lord had shown me. I had lain on the lonely altar when I accepted that I might never be healed. I knew the pain of my heart being torn out at that acceptance.

On her long journey, Much Afraid had found a tiny flower growing in the cracks of the parched land. How it survived in the desert, she couldn't tell. She bent low and whispered, "What is your name?"

"Acceptance-With-Joy," the tiny bloom answered.

I had accepted; but for me, there was no joy. All I had was determination.

∽

Chapter 13

∽

Confidence

DURING JANUARY OF the fourth year, I kept going back to that list of names. I prayed and confessed the personality traits that had grown out of my old names and asked God how I could become the person these new names described.

Brass Nugget 23: Finding Confidence

By late March, I had not made much progress. Alone in the ironing room, I turned back, as I had done so many times, to the page where I had written the list of old names. I began yet again to ask the Lord for insight as to how I could overcome my defects.

For a moment or two, I sat staring at the page where I had listed the old names. It dawned on me that I had not looked at the list of new names for months. I flicked back through the pages but couldn't find the one with the new names. I was sure I had listed them on a separate page. I looked back further, then flipped forward again. But no, I had not recorded them.

I was puzzled. I had often sung the song about them in the car, in the shower, while I ironed, but I hadn't made a note of them.

I selected a pen, smoothed my hand across a fresh page, and wrote:

> Confidence
> Joyfulness
> Overcoming one
> Faithfulness
> Friend of God
> One who seeks His Face.

I read aloud softly, but as I reached the last two names, my voice strengthened, and I felt a stirring in my spirit. I thought, "These two are the most important. They shouldn't be written last. I'll write the list again, putting them first."

> One who seeks His Face
> Friend of God
> Faithfulness
> Overcoming one
> Joyfulness
> Confidence

That's when I saw the list as a ladder or a stairway. I saw the first name, Confidence, as the bottom step. Somehow I knew that once I attained that, the others would follow in natural order. I thanked the Lord He had given me a plan: I needed to build confidence. That seemed logical to me.

In the past, I had been very self-assured. To dance before hundreds of people had once been as easy and natural as breathing. Now, I had no confidence at all, especially in social settings. Welcoming people into my own home made me tremble with fear. I would hide in the kitchen and send James to welcome our guests. I could only enter the room full of visitors if I carried a tray of canapés to offer them, holding it like a protective barrier.

My husband wasn't aware of these struggles, and I doubt the guests ever suspected, for I worked hard to remain in control. But the anguish was real, and I had to deal with it on a regular basis. I was tired of pretending. I prayed, "Lord, make it real, make me real. I want reality Christianity!"

One of the first verses I had written in my original notebook was, "In quietness and in confidence is your strength" (Isaiah 30:15 TLB). I thought if I could regain my confidence, I could get better.

During one prayer time, I suddenly understood it was not *self*-confidence I needed, but *God*-confidence. I began to truthfully thank the Lord that there was nothing left of the old me, and asked Him to fill me with Himself, to re-build me His way.

I knew that this reliance on the Lord would not be established overnight, for it would involve a total change in my thought life. I decided to give this year a name, "My Year of Confidence."

As I wrote that heading at the top of a new page, the thought came to me that the metallurgical process of extracting iron from stones is lengthy, requiring rocks containing the iron ore to be crushed and then suffer the intense heat of the smelting furnace before the pure, liquid iron flows. I hoped that in this year I would grow confident in the Lord and so extract some iron from my stones.

Brass Nugget 24: Submission or Acceptance

About the middle of the year, as I sat praying with my Bible open and my notes scattered around me, the Holy Spirit spoke to my heart. *What is the difference between acceptance and submission?*

After puzzling for some moments, the answer came to my mind like a soft whisper: *Submission is white-knuckled resignation. Acceptance is open-handed trust.*

It was true. I *was* hanging on with sheer determination, bowed under the weight of my stones like a yoke from which there was no escape. With a heavy heart, I acknowledged that I was not practicing acceptance, but offering instead my reluctant submission.

But did understanding this change anything? I longed for release. Once again, I told the Lord I would accept, but this time, I asked Him to show me how to do it freely, without the white knuckles.

After this prayer, I felt empty. How could I possibly accept freely?

For the second time, like a whisper in my mind, came, *Father, if it is possible, may this cup be taken from me* (Matthew 26:39 NIV).

Those words sifted down to some deep place. With a sense of relief, I realized Jesus knew how I felt. He had prayed for release, but unlike me, Jesus was able to accept it. How could He do that? How could He, knowing the full horror of what lay ahead, say, "Not my will but yours be done" (Luke 22:42 NIV)? I closed my eyes and tried to envision the anguish of that moment. It was beyond imagining.

But slowly, a new insight was revealed. Jesus won the struggle as He looked into the face of His Father. His loving Father passed the cup of suffering to Him. Jesus reached out and took the cup, not reluctantly, but willingly. I gasped as I realized that knowing Who holds your suffering removes the fear from acceptance.

If I believed the hand of the enemy held the cup of suffering, I would always push it away. But knowing Jesus held that cup, I could reach out to take it—and as I did, I would touch His hand.

I wrote in my notebook: "To accept is to look up into the face of my Jesus. To accept is to receive with the open hands of trust." I found strength in those thoughts even as I wrote them.

This brass nugget took on a new sheen a few weeks later when a dear elderly lady, who knew nothing of my struggle, gave everyone in the group a copy of a poem. As I looked down at the heading on the paper she'd placed in my hand, it was as though the Lord said to me, "See, you are not alone. Down through the ages, other pilgrims have walked this path."

In Acceptance Lieth Peace
(Amy Carmichael)

He said, "I will forget the dying faces;
The empty places,
They shall be filled again.
O voices moaning deep within me cease."
But vain the word; vain, vain;
Not in forgetting lieth peace.

He said, "I will crowd action upon action,
The strife of faction
Shall stir me and sustain;
O tears that drown the fire of manhood
   cease."
But vain the word; vain, vain;
Not in endeavour lieth peace.

He said, "I will withdraw me and be quiet,
Why meddle in life's riot?
Shut be my door to pain.
Desire, thou dost befool me, thou shall
   cease."
But vain the word; vain, vain;
Not in aloofness lieth peace.

He said, "I will submit; I am defeated.
God hath depleted
My life of its rich gain.
O futile murmurings, why will ye not cease?"
But vain the word; vain, vain.
Not in submission lieth peace.

He said, "I will accept the breaking sorrow
Which God tomorrow
Will to his son explain.
Then did the turmoil deep within him cease.
Not vain the word, not vain;
For in acceptance lieth peace.[22]

I put that poem in a plastic pocket in my ring
binder, but not before I had underlined, "For in
acceptance lieth peace."

I longed to move into this deeper stage of
acceptance, but how to attain it was beyond my
understanding.

Brass Nugget 25: A Promise

I stood in a dim passage in the home of an
elderly friend and peered into her overcrowded
bookcase. Perusing other people's bookshelves had
become a habit.

One title caught my eye: *If I Open My Door* by Rita
Snowdon. I eased it from the shelf, gritty with dust.

Miniscule, spidery writing covered the flyleaf
and the facing page. I moved to the light streaming
from the sitting room to get a better look. The barely-

legible scrawls were quotations. Each involved the imagery of doorways, all quotations from authors I collected. Of all the books in the bookcase, I had reached out and chosen this one!

"May I borrow this?" I asked Joan.

"If you think you might like it," she said, "it's yours to keep."

I was delighted. The author's writing was refreshing, bringing precious truths alive in a simple, charming style. I read that book every night until I was almost at the end. Because it did not require the intense concentration that many of the old writers' works do, it was a good way to unwind.

At the end of one stressful day, I fell into bed exhausted and began to read, not expecting anything more than to read myself to sleep. But one paragraph spoke to my heart:

> In return for this utter surrender you will find He will give the peace you want most, with its joy far surpassing any fleeting patches of happiness you have known. He will give you peace of mind in place of the distraction and strain of a self-guided life. He will give you power over those miserable defects which have seemed at times almost unconquerable. He will give you an experience of abundant living. But you must be prepared for other things as well. He may take you, perhaps along a way where

some of your friends turn back, unable to face the demands of His way of life. He will not deliver you from the things men are afraid of – poverty, hardship, loneliness, suffering, death. But He will deliver you from being afraid of them. More, he will open to you opportunities for service that you've never dreamed of before. You will be tired and discouraged and ready to give in. At times it will seem to you as if the sun had gone out and as if nothing matters and nobody cares. Sometimes, the precious thing you place great store by will be misunderstood, perhaps by your close friends, and you are bound to be hurt. But despair will not seize hold of you because the task is hard and there seems to be no way out. These things aren't a scrap easy, I know. But you will sustain yourself by the proud thought that you are in the line of heroes. Behind you stand a great cloud of witnesses... you will never shame these mighty names by turning back. There is no peace in cowardice. Peace isn't tame and spiritless. Down the ages the symbol of the kingdom is not a cushion but a cross.[23]

Oh, there was so much to take in. I spent days thinking through it all. Utter surrender to the Lord would give me power to overcome my miserable defects. Utter surrender was just another way of saying acceptance.

The Lord had made it clear that if my life were to change, His way of acceptance was the only way.

Brass Nugget 26: Dianna's Example

During the months of struggling with this deeper acceptance, I received an invitation from Elizabeth to come for lunch.

When we gathered at Lady Elizabeth's for afternoon tea, we would be entertained in the conservatory or the family sitting room. But for lunch, we had the privilege of being served in the formal dining room. Whether for afternoon tea or lunch, gathering at Elizabeth's was always a treat. She loved to bless us and spared no effort in doing so. Her table was resplendent with shining silverware on a starched, damask tablecloth. Each place setting sparkled with crystal glasses and the finest porcelain.

After lunch, Elizabeth liked to show us around her garden. As we broke into twos and threes to stroll across the lawn, I found myself beside Dianna. I noticed she looked tired and asked if she was feeling ill. She turned to face me and said simply, "Just in a little pain." Then she changed the subject, and we continued down the path following the others.

The following week, Dianna's mother died. This came as a shock, as she had been reasonably fit and healthy. Dianna's father was frail, and she worried he wouldn't cope on his own, so she decided to move back home to care for him. I didn't see Dianna again until nine months later, at her father's funeral.

When she stood to speak, her face seemed to radiate the presence of the Lord. I was held by the serene beauty of her face and by the gentleness in the delivery of the few words she spoke.

Dianna returned to her seat, and a long silence followed. Then, person after person stood to tell of how they had come to know the Lord through Dianna's father and mother. Some of those former neighbours, friends, or work colleagues had travelled long distances to be there. Each spoke of two humble, unassuming people who lived in such a way as to produce in others an irresistible desire to know the Lord. What a legacy. "No wonder Dianna's so special," I thought.

At the refreshments after the funeral, I overheard a conversation.

"Dianna must have struggled through those last months, with the pain so bad."

"I hear she's on strong medication, but it doesn't really help."

"Polymyalgia Rheumatica, I think it's called."

She had a chronic illness? How could this be the first I'd heard of it? She had never complained, and whenever I had spoken with her on the phone, she spoke of how good the Lord had been to her.

Stunned by the news, I found Dianna in the crowd and took her aside. She told me simply that she had battled for years. "There has been much prayer, but… I have come to accept it now."

I drove home thinking of her shining face. Acceptance had brought her peace.

Some weeks later, Dianna gave me a copy of Amy Carmichael's *Rose from Brier* and pointed me to this paragraph:

> I have known lovers of our Lord who in their spiritual youth were sure beyond a doubt that healing would always follow the prayer of faith and the anointing of oil in the name of the Lord. But those same dear lovers, in their beautiful maturity, passed through illness, unrelieved by any healing. And when I looked in wonder, remembering all that they had held and taught in other years, I found them utterly at rest. The secret of their Lord was with them. He had said to them, their own beloved Lord had said it, 'Let not your heart be troubled, neither let it be afraid,' so their hearts were not troubled or afraid, and their song was always of the loving-kindness of the Lord. 'As for God, his way is perfect,' they said. 'We need no explanation.'[24]

Brass Nugget 27: Not the End of the Story

Most mornings after James and the children had left, I would make a pot of tea and retreat to the ironing room, my small sanctuary. The battered old chair had become so bathed in prayer that often, as I lowered myself into it, I'd feel the Lord's love enfold me.

On one such morning, I opened my Bible to the daily reading. Moses was speaking to the Israelites.

"I will die in this land; I will not cross the Jordan; but you are about to cross over and take possession of that good land" (Deuteronomy 4:22 NIV).

How hard it must have been for Moses, seeing the Promised Land so near yet knowing he would never reach it. Such sadness, such bitter disappointment, never to know the fulfilment of his life's journey.

A few weeks later, while reading Matthew, there came a sudden insight.

I had read Matthew 17 many times, yet had missed a tiny detail. When Jesus was transfigured on the mountain, two others stood with Him, Elijah and Moses. I knew that passage well, yet I had never before comprehended the phrase *and Moses*.

Moses stood in the land he had not been able to reach in his earthly life, and he stood there with the long-promised Messiah. Moses now had fulfilment beyond measure, with all the disappointments of his earthly life long forgotten.

Though I saw a glimpse of eternity in this new insight, it aroused difficult questions. Could *I* accept delayed fulfilment? Could I live for heaven?

I didn't like the answer my shallow heart gave. For me, delayed fulfilment was not good enough.

A few weeks later, a new understanding of another familiar passage prodded me with those same questions:

> These men of faith I have mentioned died without ever receiving all that God had promised them; but they saw it all awaiting them on ahead and were glad, for they agreed that this earth was not their real home but that they were just strangers visiting down here. And quite obviously when they talked like that, they were looking forward to their real home in heaven." (Hebrews 11:13-14 TLB)

On previous readings, I'd missed the breathtaking sweep of the passage. I had been led to believe we should keep praying and never give up until we receive what we asked for; but these men *never* received!

I read through the list of names in Hebrews 11: Enoch, Noah, Abraham, Moses. These men received some, but not all, of the promises. In their earthly lives, they never fulfilled their dreams. These men lived in anticipation of their eternal inheritance.

How were they able to keep their focus on eternity? What was their secret? Could I learn to live in the same, radically different, way?

The sermon on the following Sunday was from 2 Corinthians 4.

It had become my practice to take notes while

listening to a sermon. Some Sundays I wrote pages, others just a line or two. That morning I wrote only two words, "Verse 18." Late that evening, when I had time to myself, I opened my Bible and read:

> So we fix our eyes not on what is seen,
> but on what is unseen, since what is seen
> is temporary, but what is unseen is
> eternal. (2 Corinthians 4:18 NIV)

As I read that verse, an idea impressed itself upon my mind...

I held an old-fashioned telescope. I closed one eye and peered into the eyepiece with the other. The far horizon, formerly dimmed by distance, now came into sharp focus. I heard the Holy Spirit whisper, "You need to close one eye to the world so you are able to focus on the treasures I have stored up for you."

I pondered that thought for some time, then wrote in my journal, "Christians are designed to live with their eyes fixed on eternity."

And then in large letters, "Earth is not meant to be a heavenly paradise free from pain and suffering."

Brass Nugget 28: Hope

We stood at the graveside. The words "In the sure and certain hope of the resurrection" were whipped away by the wind. The faces of those who grieved were taut with loss, for they did not believe.

For them, death meant the end. Someone released balloons, and we watched as the wind caught them.

On the way home, I thought about the reading at the graveside, "In the sure and certain hope of the resurrection." *Sure and certain.* Those words soar with confidence. Yet the next word, *hope*, seems to come down with a sinking feeling. It seemed *hope* suggested not certainty, but wishful thinking.

After church the next Sunday, I asked my minister about the word. He indicated that *hope* no longer carries the same connotation as it once did. Today we say something like, *I hope it will not rain on the weekend.* To hope means to wish for something, conveying no certainty or assurance.

Yet the original meaning of the word hope is *excited anticipation.*

Hundreds of years ago, a young boy might have said, "I am hoping for my birthday," meaning he couldn't wait! He knew for certain his birthday was coming, and he was excited about it. So the phrase "sure and certain hope" means sure and certain, excited anticipation of the resurrection.

Wow, excited anticipation! After explaining this, my minister smiled. I thanked him and sipped my coffee. But as he walked away, I realized I was not excited about heaven. Yes, I believed in eternal life. But the thought of delayed fulfilment brought a dull ache of longing for release NOW.

Later, as I flicked through my notes to find a reference, I stopped at Isaiah 54:11, "Thou afflicted, tossed with tempest, not comforted! I will set your stones in antimony to enhance their brilliance" (DBY).

I had written out the whole verse and scribbled underneath, Stones = difficulties. Antimony = darkness.

I glanced at the date on the top of the page. Three and a half years had passed. I was supposed to have spent that time shining in the darkness, but I had not. I was still a crabby, prickly woman when pushed too hard.

I prayed, "Lord, I long to yield to You, so Your nature can shine through me. How long will it take until I can surrender to You utterly?" Moments passed, and as I opened my eyes, I saw the next line of that verse.

"I will lay your foundations with sapphires."

What did *that* mean? Having learned not to brush aside difficult verses as simply poetic language, I looked more closely. A foundation is that which is built upon. But sapphires?

After racing to the bookshelf, I cleared a place on the ironing board for the heavy Strong's concordance and flipped through to S, quickly scanning down to "sapphire." The first reference was Exodus 24:10: "and they saw [a manifestation of] the God of Israel; and under His feet there appeared to be a pavement of sapphire, just as clear as the sky itself" (AMP).

Sapphire represents heaven! My life is to be built on thoughts of my eternal home. I knelt before my chair and buried my head in the cushion. *Lord, I want to live with my eyes fixed, not on the things of Earth but, on my eternal future.*

Each day, my prayers now ended with thoughts of my eternal inheritance. I wrote, "Take the long view. Run for the finish line."

Brass Nugget 29: Stop Wishing It Was Lighter

Now that I no longer taught ballet six days a week, weight crept on, pound after pound. I promised myself I would exercise. But, lacking motivation, I needed a group setting. I'd have preferred a senior ballet class, but as none was available close to home, I joined a gym, thinking that at least aerobics classes would be familiar—mirrors, music, and someone out in front shouting instructions.

I still wondered how I would be able to do all that the Lord was asking of me. How could I be gentle, kind, loving and forgiving, even under pressure, with no trace of self-pity or resentment? I understood in theory, but in practice I stumbled and fell.

While at the gym one morning, I saw some men with huge muscles lifting enormous weights. As I watched, the Lord spoke into my heart, "How did these men become so strong? It wasn't by looking at the heavy weights and wishing they were lighter. No, it was by lifting them, taking them up, and bearing the weight of them. And not just once, but over and over, in a daily discipline of exercise that builds muscle and strength. If you are to be strong, you will have to take up your cross and follow Me. Stop wishing it were lighter."

I left the gym that day with a lot to think about. It made sense. I would grow by bearing the weight of life's difficulties in a godly manner. This could not be an intellectual exercise. It would have to be worked out physically in the everyday details of my life, moment by moment.

But it had taken every ounce of my will power to get this far. How could I keep trying to overcome when my efforts had already sapped my strength?

By this time, though, I'd learned one important lesson: if I did not immediately act on each new brass nugget, I would stop moving forward. In fact, I would slip back, for a rudder can only steer a ship that is moving.

Springs in the Valley provided the next brass nugget that showed me how to carry my burden.

> You are bound to a cross, I entreat
> you not to struggle, for the more
> lovingly the cross is carried by the
> soul, the lighter it becomes.[25]

I prayed over and over, "Lord show me how to bear my cross lovingly."

Brass Nugget 30: Graceful

I realize that I have often written, "the Lord said to me," and I don't feel comfortable about that. It makes me sound as if I'm some sort of special person with a hotline to heaven, when in reality, I'm a stumbling follower of Jesus. Precious nuggets didn't come every time I sat to pray. Day followed heavy day with no special word, just the discipline of reading, praying, waiting, and writing.

In my previous Christian life, when I had been strong and sure of myself, words from the Lord were rare indeed. Now, desperately clinging to Jesus, I was able to hear Him. It was never an audible voice, but His words flowed through my mind—peaceful, loving, at times startling, but always wise beyond anything I could think. Nearly every time He spoke, it was with a bewildering question to which I had no answer.

The next such question was, "What does it mean to be graceful?"

I thought for some minutes. Then I said, "Well, Lord, grace in ballet is the art of making the difficult appear effortless." Then the next question came: "How do you do that?"

In an instant I understood.

In ballet, the only way to attain grace is through pain. The muscles must be stretched, and stretching is painful. When teaching, I encouraged young students to hold the stretch at the pain point for a few seconds and not pull back, for that is the point where the muscle is lengthened. Each time this is done, the muscle will stretch further, until eventually there is no resistance. Once the limb moves without restriction, grace is achieved.

It takes about fifteen years to train a dancer. Fifteen years of daily stretching to the point of pain in order to achieve freedom of movement and gracious liberty.

The Lord had already shown me I needed to strengthen my "spiritual muscles." Now, I understood I must stretch to the pain point—and hold it. Yet I feared the pain point. Each time the tender places of my heart were strained, I pulled back to what felt comfortable to me.

Then came a humbling thought: forgiveness stretched the Father to the point of pain. Though it cost Him His Son, He did not pull back.

A few weeks later, I read Philippians 1:9, "…may your love abound more and more…" (NIV).

The Lord whispered, "Why does a dancer push through the pain?"

Oh, I saw it. We push through for love. For the passionate love of dance and the dream of grace.

I said, "Lord, I want to love You with more passion than I ever felt for dance. For the love of You, I will push through and catch the vision of the life of grace."

Brass Nugget 31: White Linen

Ena did all the family's ironing except for James' white shirts. He was very particular about the collars, as they were seen above his court robes.

He liked his shirts to be one hundred percent heavyweight cotton, which made them difficult to iron. Even the powerful shooting steam of the commercial iron was no match for them. I had to spray the shirts with water and stretch them while I pressed down as hard as I could, and at the same time, continuously push the button to release bursts of high-pressure steam.

Five crinkled shirts lay in the laundry basket. I sprayed them all with water to soften them and then arranged the first on the ironing board, preparing to do battle.

Ssshhh went the steam. With it, "Without stain or wrinkle," ssshhhed into my mind.

I knew those words were in one of Paul's letters, but which one? I pulled the heavy Strong's Concordance from the bookshelf and settled into my chair. The ironing could wait.

I found it in Ephesians 5:26-27: "...to make her holy, cleansing her by the washing with water through the word, and to present her to himself as a radiant church *without stain or wrinkle* or any other blemish, but holy and blameless" (NIV).

I had been washed by Jesus' sacrifice; but I was not all I should be...there were wrinkles left. Kaye and I had often spoken about the "pressures" of life, and I had read the phrase "the heat of suffering." I opened my ring binder and wrote, "To be clothed in 'white linen without stain or wrinkle,' I need to be ironed. There is no way to remove wrinkles but by heat and pressure."

I put the ring binder away and went back to the shirts. As I sprayed the first with water, I had another "aha!" moment. Without water to soften the fibres, no amount of heat and pressure will smooth out the wrinkles. The analogy was obvious: I needed to be soaked in the word of God—wet right through—to become soft enough to allow Jesus to stretch me under the heat and pressure of my difficulties.

Every day, I immersed myself in Paul's Epistle to the Philippians. It became my textbook on how to stretch spiritually. I copied large chunks of it into my notebook. These verses (all quoted below in the NIV) were my daily practice routine:

Phil 1:27: "Whatever happens, conduct yourselves in a manner worthy of the gospel of Christ."

Phil 2:14: "Do everything without grumbling or arguing so that you will become blameless and pure."

Phil 4:5: "Let your gentleness be evident to all."

I usually skimmed over the beginning and the end of Paul's letters; the list of greetings and the unpronounceable names did not make for interesting reading. But one morning I happened to read the end of Philippians 4:22, "...those who belong to Caesar's household."

That stopped me mid-sentence. There were Christians in Caesar's household! In such an ungodly place, it was unlikely they were there by choice—most likely, they were slaves. I looked at the whole of Philippians from a new perspective. Paul wrote to encourage those whose stones were much heavier than mine. This realization renewed my determination to practice in my everyday life all God had shown me so far, and so keep the passion and the dream of grace alive.

Brass Nugget 32: Do Not Pull Back

James felt the approaching holiday might be his elderly mother's last Christmas, and he wanted all the extended family to be together. So he invited his mother, brother and sister, their children, and various aunts, uncles and cousins—fourteen people in all—to spend Christmas with the five of us. They planned to arrive Christmas Eve and, as some travelled long distances and had not seen each other for years, they were to stay ten days.

I went weak at the knees at the very thought. How on earth could I do this? How many gallons of milk would we need? How many loaves of bread? How big a turkey? Three meals a day for ten days for nineteen people!

It wasn't just the practical things that loomed before me, but the thought of spending so much time with my husband's family. I felt uncomfortable around them, for they were a socially prominent family, and I had convinced myself they thought I was not good enough for them.

Despair crept up on me. It was hopeless. I could never do it. But I resigned myself to it, and so I trudged on into December.

The house echoed with Christmas carols and children's laughter as we brought the Christmas decorations down from the attic. The children helped decorate the formal dining room and sitting room. Garlands of spruce boughs graced the mantelpieces, tied in the corners with shimmering organza bows. The tree touched the ceiling, so I needed a ladder to reach the top while the children decorated the lower branches.

Two hours later, the tree shone. Gilded angels, hearts, doves, and wise men on camels glittered in the fairy lights. I stood back to admire my handiwork, then rearranged some of the children's contributions. Once satisfied, I moved to the entrance hall and called the children, but their enthusiasm for decorating had waned. The spruce garlands, baskets of pinecones, cinnamon sticks, and red velvet ribbons were in the middle of the hall, but the children were nowhere to be seen. When I called again, only echoes replied.

Ordinarily, I loved decorating for Christmas, but this year, the enormity of all that lay ahead weighed me down. If you've suffered from depression, you know how real and debilitating the physical exhaustion can be. Nevertheless, I managed to complete each item on my extensive list, so by the end of the weekend, everything was ready.

At the end of a long day, I crept into each of the children's rooms in turn, careful not to make a sound. It was too dark to see, but the steady breathing confirmed they were finally asleep. I walked back along the upstairs hall. James' study door was shut, and I heard him pacing up and down, dictating into his voice recorder. Then his chair creaked as he lowered himself into it. He was working on a difficult case, so I didn't disturb him but quietly passed the study and tiptoed down the stairs to the sitting room, where I flopped into a chair.

I thought, "This time next week, it will be Christmas Eve, and all James' family will be here. Oh, how will I make it through ten whole days with them? I wish I could just go to sleep and not wake up until it's all over."

The room was dark except for the warm flickering of the fire and the soft lights of the Christmas tree. The old house creaked, a log released a gentle hiss, but no other sound broke the stillness. Gradually, the silence filled me, and the Lord spoke gently into my heart: "They are all coming to celebrate together. Give them this Christmas as a gift.

Don't pull back. Give out. Be gracious. Don't look in at yourself and all it will cost you. Look at them through My eyes. Choose to bless."

I said, "Yes, Lord, I will."

Over the next few days leading up to the family's arrival, each time I began to panic, I would say, "I will give it as a gift because You ask it, Lord." I was stretched to the pain point and didn't pull back; and each time, I was able to go a little further.

During those hectic days, Philippians 1:9 kept coming back to my mind: "May your love abound more and more..." (NIV). I was learning to look at others through Jesus' eyes—to let Him love them through me. Jesus gave me this motto: SEEK TO BLESS, NOT IMPRESS. If I panicked, it was because I was looking in at myself and feeling inadequate instead of looking out and giving out, loving and blessing.

That Christmas marked the beginning of my training in grace. I practiced welcoming all who came to our home as guests of the Lord. I was learning to carry my cross lovingly—and, to my surprise, it grew lighter.

As the New Year approached, it seemed logical to call the coming year after the next name on the ladder, Joyfulness. I was now willing for God to stretch me, but there had to be more. I longed for the "joy of my salvation."

∞

Chapter 14

∞

Joyfulness

THIS WAS TO be my year of growing in joy—but joy still eluded me.

I had deep concerns for my boys. What would become of them? Would they go down the same path as their father? Would they inherit a predisposition for alcoholism? I prayed for them, but I feared I lacked whatever it took to set captives free. Though I had confidence in the Lord, I had none in my own ability to do spiritual warfare.

Brass Nugget 33: It Is Not Dependent On Me!

The morning rush was over. I headed into the ironing room and sank the chair. As I picked up my Bible, the bookmark dropped out. I flipped through Isaiah to find my place. As I turned the pages, Isaiah 49:24 caught my eye: "Can plunder be taken from warriors, or captives be rescued from the fierce" (NIV)?

I held my breath. That was what I'd just thought! My heart pounded as I read the next two verses.

"But this is what the Lord says: Yes, captives will be taken from warriors, and plunder retrieved from the fierce. I will contend with those who contend with you, and your children I will save" (Isaiah 49:25 NIV).

I will contend with those who contend with you.

I was stunned. It took some moments for that truth to sink in. *It was not dependent on me!*

God was fighting for me. He had everything under control.

A weight lifted from my shoulders. I was confident in God.

I was confident in God! I was *confident* in God!!

Picking up that nugget lifted me to a new level.

But then, a new and massive stone came crashing into my life. Alistair, my ex-husband, asked to see the boys. They'd longed for this, but for years, we didn't know his whereabouts. Now he was back in the area, and the boys were excited to see him.

Suddenly, every other weekend they were out of my care and with a man whose lifestyle was shocking. He had long since left the woman he had run off with and, after a succession of partners, was with a very strange woman. The first time I saw her, dressed totally in black, with dyed hair, tattoos, and heavy eye makeup, I was afraid for my boys. I worried about the things they would see and the influences they would come under, but they were now thirteen and sixteen, which made them legally old enough to choose.

Alistair lived in the inner city and gave the boys unlimited freedom. No rules, no homework, no accountability. They wandered about at will. Friends saw them in the streets late at night. When first David chose to live with his father and, shortly after, Peter followed, it tore out my heart. Only a mother whose children have been taken from her can know the anguish of the days and nights of wondering if they were safe.

Every second weekend when the boys came home, I noticed signs of neglect. I had been able to trust them to Jesus' care two days out of fourteen, but their being away twelve days out of fourteen made it far more difficult. I wanted to trust, but constantly slipped back into fear.

All the advances I had made were swallowed up in worry for my children.

Brass Nugget 34: Take Every Thought Captive

I love to mow the lawn. Sitting on the ride-on mower, I can think and pray, all while doing something practical that requires no physical effort.

One afternoon, with the late spring sunshine warm on my back, I talked to the Lord. "I seem to be just plodding along. I'm determined to follow You, but I don't seem to be making much headway. How can I move on?"

A gentle whisper came: "Take every thought captive and make it subject to Christ."

Every thought! How could anyone ever take *every* thought captive? My first reaction was, "That's impossible. I could never do it!" But there came a quiet urging in my spirit that stilled those doubts, and there in the sun, I prayed that I would be open to this even if it seemed impossible. As I put the lawn mower away, I reasoned if the word of God asked me to do it, then it must be possible. So as an act of faith, I began.

At first I could only catch one thought a day, or maybe two. But I slowly got better at it. I found to my surprise that when I was not consciously thinking, a constant jumble of thoughts, words, ideas, and worries played in my mind like continual background music. I learned to grab one of those tumbling thoughts and hold it as though I'd pressed a pause button, and then I could examine it carefully.

I was shocked at what I found. When not concentrating on something in particular, my mind replayed old hurts, fears, and failures. It fed on them like poison, and I did not even know it was happening. Sometimes these thoughts were painful; sometimes I could hardly believe the blackness or the bitterness. I cried out to the Lord to help me deal with what I was finding. Then I realized I was only doing the first part of the verse; I was taking the thought captive, but I was not making it obedient to Christ.

How was I to do that? I gradually came to see that each time I caught a destructive thought, I needed to replace it with one of the brass nuggets the Lord had already given me. A snippet of a verse I'd jotted in my first notebook came to mind: "…His faithful promises are my armor…" (Psalm 91:4 TLB).

I went back through my notebook and made a list of every nugget that was a promise. I typed out that list and carried it in my handbag so I could take it out and read it often, even in line at the supermarket.

"I will contend with those who contend with you and your children I will save" (Isaiah 49:25-26 NIV).

"Again I will build you and you will be strong" (Jeremiah 31:4 NASB).

"I will replace the years that the locusts have eaten" (Joel 2:25 NJKV).

"The Lord is close to the broken hearted and saves those who are crushed in spirit" (Psalm 34:18 NIV).

"I will make the vale of sorrow a door of hope" (Hosea 2:15 MNT).

These promises had strengthened me in the past. They were His faithful promises! And so I began using these nuggets as armour. When I stood behind them, they made my thoughts obedient to Christ.

At this point, I found it all too easy to fall into the mistake of simply saying the words. If I repeated them often enough, they became meaningless. I needed to dwell on the beauty of the One Who gave me the words. Only then did those scriptures shine as love notes of the Spirit.

Fear of the future was defeated by "stones are iron." I told myself, "The future holds no terrors. If more stones come into my life, God will use them to further strengthen me." This took decided effort, but I learned to reject fear and worry.

One day during the first few months of taking captive fears and worries, I drove home by a different route and saw a large sign outside a church that read, "Worry is the darkroom where negatives are developed."

As soon as I was home, I wrote that in my ring binder and under it I wrote: "Worry robs joy. Do not worry."

I told the Lord I would trust Him. I would trust Him even if my boys never came back. I wrote, truly believing that I meant it, "Though He slay me yet will I praise Him" (Job 13:15 NKJV).

The truth of this statement was soon to be tested.

Brass Nugget 35: Reach for the Finish Line

After many months of trying to "take every thought captive," to replace negative thoughts with my precious nuggets, I had taken much ground from the enemies in my heart. The panic attacks were less frequent, and I possessed a new strength.

My boys, David and Peter, had spent the weekend at home with me. We had a wonderful time rowing around the lake and picnicking on a small island. The boys took their tent and camped out there overnight. Claire insisted she was big enough to camp out too, but the boys didn't want a little sister to look after. I only managed to get her back in the dingy by promising we would sleep in a tent close to the house. We did—but sharing a camp mattress with a small child who kicked and wriggled meant I slept very little that night.

On Sunday evening, David and Peter packed to go back to the city and their father. James was to drive them. But Claire made a fuss. She didn't want to be left behind, so James strapped her in the car seat for the long drive. As I hugged my boys good-bye, I was amazed to find the pit of my stomach free from the usual gnawing pain. I truly trusted the Lord to take care of them.

I watched until the car turned the corner at the end of the lane, then strolled through the garden enjoying the golden light of late afternoon and a new, quiet peace. Under a spreading elm I stopped to whisper a prayer of thanks. Love encompassed me. The presence of the Lord seemed right beside me, real and tangible. Peace, love, and strength wrapped gentle arms around me. I relaxed into His beautiful presence for a moment.

But then, with a sharp intake of breath, I remembered that twice before, when I had felt His lovely presence with this same intensity, it was just before a tragedy.

Fear gripped me. His presence meant an imminent disaster! For some inexplicable reason, I felt that disaster was the death of our little Claire. It was as though this was already a fact. "No! Not my little girl! Don't take my little girl!" I rang James' phone, but got no answer.

Gripped with terror, I ran inside and flung myself face-down in my prayer chair, sobbing. I shook uncontrollably, pleading with God to spare my daughter's life. "No! Not this! Please not this! Haven't I suffered enough?"

I don't know how long I cried and pleaded, terrified, ringing James' mobile again and again, but he never picked up. As each minute passed, the terror intensified.

As carefully as my shaking allowed, I weighed all I had learned: This life is not all there is; we have eternity. Even if God takes her, I will see her in heaven. The sorrow of loss is only for a time. "Do I believe that?" I sobbed. "Do I really believe that? If I believe there is eternal life, then I can face this."

Could I, though? Could I accept even this?

With an enormous effort of will, I pushed myself up from my knees and stood, shaking, tears streaming down my face, and forced out the words, "Let the axe fall. The deal still stands. I will still love You."

I was so weak I went to bed. I pulled the quilt up over my head and lay there, numb, too exhausted to think. I must have dozed, for my ringing phone woke me. I answered, and through the sleep haze I heard James' voice. All was well. Claire was safe.

For many days after, I didn't notice a difference in myself. But as the weeks passed, I realized the panic attacks and the vague, senseless fear were gone.

The Lord had allowed fear to come to its zenith. I believe the enemy had gambled on me turning back. Writing this now, my words seem hopelessly inadequate to convey what happened that day, the change from intense fear to an indescribable release that followed my acceptance of God's will, whatever it may bring.

I firmly believe that had my fears been realized, though the pain would have devastated me, I would not have fallen back into the black well of depression and despair. Somehow, weak and gasping, I had reached my hand across the finish line.

∽

Chapter 15

∽

Overcoming One

SIX YEARS HAD passed since the gentle unfolding of "whose stones are iron and in whose hills you may dig brass." I was now stronger, able to go further, but my circumstances were no easier. With every advance, the situation seemed to worsen: more pressures piled upon me, more people to deal with, more stress.

Were these circumstances an attack of the enemy to keep me from moving on? "I will contend with those who contend with you" was a powerful, life-changing nugget, yet often I found myself trying to cover all the bases in prayer, falling back to a mindset of battling. Day by day, I needed to re-learn the same lessons of rest and trust.

Brass Nugget 36: Training

I picked up one of the two bulging, tattered ring binders from beside my Bible and leafed through the pages crammed with scribbles. In large letters at the top of one page, I had written, "What does it mean to be graceful? The difficult made to appear effortless."

I closed my eyes, remembering my training...the effort; the long hours of practice at the *barre*, the stretching, the aching muscles. And in that moment I knew—yes, *knew*—that this increase in pressure, these trying circumstances, were not attacks of the enemy, but training exercises of the Lord!

Why had I not seen it before? I did exactly the same thing when training young dancers. I began with the basics, and as soon as the simple exercises are perfected, moved them on to something more challenging. Progressing to a higher level often makes the young students feel they are going backwards instead of forwards. But if dancers stay at a level they're comfortable with and are not challenged, they cannot fulfil their potential. In the same way, if I were to grow in God, I had to be challenged.

The Lord reminded me of the daunting challenge of pointe shoes. Young dancers dream of floating across the stage *en pointe*, but the dream quickly becomes a nightmare. The satin pointe shoes are hard and unyielding, painful blisters form, and steps perfected by years of training seem almost impossible. But once the shoes are mastered, they become a means of grace.

Ballet teachers have sayings to reflect this: the pain you feel today is the strength you will feel tomorrow; you have to get blisters to get better; make friends with pain; and push through.

I realized now that God cared about me too much to let me stay at my comfort level. To grow in grace, I would have to get blisters.

Brass Nugget 37: Gifted

I remembered the incredibly gifted students I'd had the privilege of teaching—beautiful young dancers, artistic, sensitive, full of promise. Because I loved them and wanted them to achieve, I challenged them. But I was always careful to not break them by giving them more than they could bear. In the same way, Jesus tenderly considered each new level of my training.

I wrote in my notes, "Truly these stresses and strains are the carefully planned training exercises of the Lord."

With my pen poised above the paper, a new insight took my breath away. When ballet students are particularly gifted, more careful attention is paid to their training. The gifted ones are pushed harder than their less talented peers; more is expected, because the teacher can see the student's great potential.

We are all gifted students! We have the gift of the Holy Spirit indwelling us. God sees in us all the potential to be trained into the likeness of His Son, and He is not about to give up on us. I wrote, "Lord I will not resist Your training. I will trust that You know what You are doing."

Over the weeks that followed, I found so many ballet analogies that I could hardly believe I'd never seen them before.

As a trained dancer, I knew all the techniques required to teach others. Even though I had not danced professionally for years, I could walk into a studio and teach the most advanced and difficult movements, correct the tiniest technical fault. I could explain in great detail how it should be done, but as I was not practicing, I could no longer do it myself.

Lord, forgive my unbelief! All the scriptural knowledge crammed into my head had been unable to help me through these hard years. I knew the technique of the Christian life in theory, but had not been actively practicing it. To be all I longed to be, I needed to do more than hold scripture in my head. I needed to allow Jesus to have His way.

Oswald Chambers says:

> If we obey the Spirit of God and practice in our physical life what God has put in us by His Spirit, then when the crisis comes, we shall find that our own nature as well as the grace of God will stand by us.[26]

That said it all. It is always difficult, and living it out in reality, not mere theory, requires practice. Many times I failed that year, but I followed the wisdom of an old teacher of mine. She used to say the difference between those who succeed in dance and those who give up is in how they view failure.

Her formula was E=O4C.

Error Equals Opportunity for Correction.

Each time you fail, consider: Why did you fail? What you can learn from the experience that will help you perfect your technique? I began to apply that formula to my many spiritual failures and found it was always some small thing that led to my downfall. Had I allowed myself to fall into self-pity? Had I longed for the applause of men instead of seeking to please Jesus? Was I trusting Him for the future, or beginning to worry? Had I allowed the hustle and bustle of life to encroach upon quality time with the Lord? If I honestly examined my heart, I could usually find the reason behind the failure.

I was encouraged by the verse, "Be confident in this, that He who began a good work in you will carry it through to completion" (Philippians 1:6 NIV).

I knew it was God who had begun this work in my life, for I could not have taken one step on my own. Therefore I could be confident He would complete what He had begun.

Did I expect to perfect this dance of life without sweat, self-sacrifice, and constant practice? No, of course not! I knew the dedication, grit, and determination it took to dance with grace—the grace of the difficult made to appear effortless.

Dancers love to work hard. We sit in the dressing room, dripping with sweat, and smile to each other, saying, "Wasn't that a great class?" It is joy for a dancer to labour to overcome some technical difficulty.

> Consider it pure joy, my brothers, when
> you face trials of many kinds, because
> you know that the testing of your faith
> produces perseverance. Let perseverance
> finish its work so that you may be mature
> and complete, not lacking anything
> (James 1:2-5 NIV).

I now saw those verses from James in the light of a hard class. The difficulties of life were for teaching and training, to develop in me the character God wants—the strong family resemblance to His Son.

~

Chapter 16

~

Faithfulness

I NAMED THE seventh year my year of Faithfulness.

If life moved along in a quiet, ordered pattern, I was able to remain in control. But there were often unexpected visitors, late nights, or quick changes of plans that could leave my head spinning. I longed to move into this new name, to be faithful and steady.

As I prayed about this, another ballet analogy came to mind. Pirouettes require hours of practice. Spinning on the spot leaves an untrained person off balance, but a professional dancer never becomes dizzy even when performing multiple pirouettes. To maintain balance, dancers fix their eyes on one spot at the beginning of the turn, and before the body has completed the turn, the head flicks around to fix on that same spot once again. The eyes see only that one point and so convince the brain the body is still. This prevents dizziness.

In the same way, I needed to focus on Jesus as the one unmoving point in my life in order to maintain my spiritual balance.

I could see the analogy, but maintaining the focus seemed impossible.

Brass Nugget 38: The Fixed Focus

James' ninety-two-year-old mother fell twice in six months, with the last time resulting in a broken hip. We could delay no longer: the time had come for her to move into a nursing home. The task of preparing the family home for sale was huge, and, as my husband's extended family lived far away, the chore fell to me.

Articles of furniture, paintings, and family silver were to be sent all over the country to various family members. Items no one wanted were to be auctioned. Cupboards and chests crammed with the flotsam and jetsam of generations must be opened. The contents needed to be examined, for there could be treasure in boxes that seemed to be nothing but junk. Days dragged; estate agents, auctioneers, and movers came and went. At the end of each of those long days, I sat among the boxes, exhausted. Finally, the last load was gone, and the house contained only the items we would keep. Doug, our gardener, arrived with a truck to get them.

While he loaded the items, I sat on a pile of boxes in the drive to enjoy a well-deserved cup of tea.

Relieved that the hard work was over, I stretched out and closed my eyes.

Then I almost dropped my cup with a sudden thought. The cellar! James had made it a point to remind me to check it. I hopped up and hurried to the rear of the house, where James had told me I would find the cellar door set into the foundation. It took me some time to locate it, as it was hidden by shrubbery.

After finding it, I pushed my way through, but the door was jammed. Ivy crawled over it, sealing it shut. I found Doug, and he tore away the ivy and wrenched the door open. Cobwebs stretched and broke, and dank-smelling air wafted through the opening. The flashlight's beam touched crates, broken chairs, a bicycle wheel, shelves loaded with paint cans and jars.

Doug grunted as he emerged from the dark. "Nothing but rubbish. Just leave it. Whoever buys the house can deal with it."

I took the flashlight and leaned in. The light slid over the dust of years. Yes, nothing but rubbish. But there in a corner, under a pile of wooden crates, was a trunk. I hesitated. "Get that for me, will you, Doug?"

He crouched and disappeared into the gloom, then backed out, dragging a battered tin trunk. The dust was thick and the lid stuck fast. He pried on it with a screwdriver.

The lid creaked open, and the odour of old books made Doug pull back. "Whew! What a stink!"

But to me, the odour was incense. I leaned in for a better look and stared in amazement.

On top of neat piles of books, all amazingly dust-free, sat a framed Bible verse, "The Lord shall guide thee continually" (Isaiah 58:11 KJV). Beneath the verse, in large gold-edged letters, "So do not worry."

Those words were just what I needed to hear. Beneath the frame was *The Imitation of Christ* by Thomas à Kempis, in near-perfect condition. I had been searching for a copy of this book. Beneath that lay another treasure—an anthology of the works of William Law, John Wesley's mentor.

One by one, I carefully removed the items. Sitting on my heels there on the lawn, it seemed too wonderful to be true—volume after volume of treasures. It was as though they had been waiting for me there in the dark, all those years.

Who had put them there? Most inscriptions were early 1900s. "To Kate and Grace, from the beloved trio," said one. I could not wait to ask my husband's mother if she knew who those people were.

Over the next few months, I worked my way through those books. The girls who met at Kaye's were eager to hear the details and to view the stash. One book blessed me more than all the others: *Abide in Christ* by Andrew Murray.

> O weak and trembling believer! First fix
> your eyes on that for which He has
> apprehended you. It is nothing less than a

life of abiding, unbroken fellowship with
Himself to which He is seeking to lift you
up…Fix your eyes on Christ. Gaze on
the love that beams in those eyes and that
asks whether you cannot trust Him, who
sought and found and brought you near,
now to keep you.[27]

There it was again, the fixed focus. It seemed
that the Lord wanted me to learn this lesson well.

Not long after the discovery of the stash, Kaye
found a wonderful little book that helped with that.

Brass Nugget 39: The Simple Life

A funny little second hand bookshop sits in a
quiet back street of our town. Books are not only on
the shelves but lie in boxes, stand in corners, and
balance, precariously, on every conceivable surface. A
light sprinkling of dust covers everything, lifting and
resettling as patrons stir the least-visited spots. The
proprietor knows us well and often will say as we
enter, "I've saved something for you. I think you'll
like it; it's got a religious touch."

With those words one day, that dear man handed
Kaye the little book *Jesus Loved Martha: The Housewife's
Contacts with Jesus*, by George Sinker, written in 1949.
It quickly became a favourite among us girls. It was
written to make "Practicing the Presence" a part of
every woman's daily life.

I grew excited as I read that tattered little book, for I had never thought about the ordinary things that Jesus would have done. Following the book's lead, each time I picked up a tea towel or a bath towel I remembered, "Jesus took a towel," and I would imagine Him kneeling to wash dirty feet. The next time I held a broom in my hands, I imagined Jesus sweeping the carpenter's shop, pondering that the King of Glory had the humility to take a broom.

Among the books from the tin trunk was a tiny volume, *Blessed Be Drudgery* by William C. Gannett.

> To all of us there come times when we
> are out of heart with ourselves and with
> all that goes to make up our lives… but
> we shall see everywhere about us, gems
> and treasure inestimable, which only wait
> to be ours by our use of them. [28]

The book encouraged the reader to do even the simplest chores as though they were being done for Jesus. This brought to the ordinary tasks a humbling reverence.

Oswald Chambers expanded on the sanctity of simple, everyday life.

> We never dream that all the time God is in the
> commonplace things and people around us. If
> we will do the duty that lies nearest, we shall see
> Him. [29]

Over the passing weeks, doing the duty that lay nearest to me brought a deep, restful peace. I came to see Jesus in a new way. I found Him practical and interested in the most mundane duties. Before Jesus took Peter off alone to ask that searching question, "Do you love me?" in John 21:15-17, He made sure these men He loved had a good hot breakfast. Jesus kindled the fire and cooked the fish with His own hands. When planning a formal dinner party or even a simple meal, I remembered Jesus had planned meals and, wonder of wonders, He cooked! With renewed strength, I welcomed all the numerous guests to our home as guests of the Lord, extending to them every courtesy I knew Jesus would wish. And as I did, the burden of entertaining was lifted from me: "For even the Son of Man did not come to be served, but to serve" (Mark 10:45 NIV). As I learned to welcome everyone as Jesus would welcome them, fear of people left me, never to return.

✺

Chapter 17

✺

Friend of God: One Who Seeks His Face

I NAMED THE eighth year of my journey One Who Seeks His Face. I determined that I would come to know the Lord more deeply by the end of the year. I prayed to be able to maintain the focus of seeking Jesus as the one fixed point in my life.

When looking back through my ring binder, I stopped at a page where I had written a quote from *The Pursuit of God* by A. W. Tozer.

> Hearts that are "fit to break" with love for the Godhead are those who have been in the Presence and have looked with opened eye upon the majesty of Deity... They were prophets, not scribes, for a scribe tells us what he was read, and the prophet tells what he has seen... The hard voice of the scribe sounds over evangelicalism, but the church waits for the tender voice of the saint who has penetrated the veil and has gazed with inward eye on the wonder that is God.[30]

173

I wanted to "gaze with inward eye." I wanted more than head knowledge.

I re-read *The Pursuit of* God, making many notes, for every page was sweet, fresh water, and I was thirsty. I couldn't get enough.

I went to the Christian bookstore and bought Tozer's *Knowledge of the Holy*, and as I read, my mind and spirit were enlarged. Through this book I came to glimpse in new ways the beauty, the wonder, the Holiness of God. It gave me an intense desire to know more of Him.

Brass Nugget 40: Just a Glance

In search of a lost receipt, I went to the drawer that was my "filing cabinet." A jumble of crumpled papers, cards, warranties, and letters made the drawer hard to open. I separated the mess into two piles, one batch to keep and the other to throw out.

I picked up a slightly crumpled sheet of what I recognized as the reading from our wedding, Song of Solomon 4:8-10. Years had passed since I'd last seen that paper. Tenderly, I smoothed it open, and a strong memory swept over me… I walk down the aisle to my bridegroom, and our eyes meet in a gaze of love that is held and held, as the world melts into nothingness. Nothing else matters at that moment. I am walking to him, and he loves me.

As I held that memory, a gentle stillness came over me, and I became aware of the Lord's presence. I continued to read the passage, and the voice of my heavenly Bridegroom spoke the words of verse 9 into my innermost being: "You have ravished my heart, my lovely one, my bride, I am overcome by one glance of your eyes" (TLB).

I felt Jesus standing like a Bridegroom, waiting for me, waiting for my eyes to meet His in that gaze of love that is held and held until the world melts into nothingness. As I return His look of love, He is overcome… overcome by my glance. My heart melts as love for my Saviour washes over me. Moments stretch, filled by His love… step by step I walk to Him. But then… I do not hold His look of love. I look away. I, who should be His and His alone, look away. I felt Jesus longing for me to look to Him to return His gaze of love.

With tears, I promised Jesus I would turn my eyes away from distractions and walk down the long aisle of my life, each day closer to Him, to my Bridegroom. I whispered, "I will not forget You. I will give you many little glances of love throughout each day."

Brass Nugget 41: Not Alone

Only a month later, at the end of our Bible study, Dianna, Helen, Kathryn, and I bowed our heads and prayed, one by one, around the circle. Being the last to pray, I ended with, "Lord, be with us as we go into the busy week ahead." As I spoke the words, an uncomfortable feeling came over me, one I couldn't begin to understand.

Throughout the next week, I often prayed those same words without thought—Lord, be with us—and each time, the same feeling came over me. The following week at our Bible study, the words formed in my mind as I prayed, but this time, I stopped them before they escaped my lips.

After the ladies left, I sat at the kitchen table, wondering. I had a sense that I had wounded the Lord, but couldn't understand how. Then Jesus gently spoke to my heart. "Child, I promised I would never leave you nor forsake you. Why do you keep asking Me for that which I have already given? I am not man, that I should lie. I do not come and go from you. I abide."

I whispered, "O Lord, how many times do You have to show me that You love me before I can grasp it? I will remember You are with me always, and I promise that I will never ask You to be with me again. Instead, I will always *thank* You for being with me."

But I wondered: if He was always with me, why didn't I always sense His presence? As soon as the question occurred to me, the answer came in an instant: I didn't always look at Him.

Just a few weeks before, I had promised to walk down the aisle of my life with my eyes gazing into His—but I wasn't doing it. Most of the time, I was totally unaware of His presence. But I wanted to be. He was with me always, and I wanted to sense Him always.

How could I maintain this awareness? How could I look, and keep on looking, until the inner eyes of my spirit rested on Him throughout the day?

I went to the Christian bookstore that very day and bought Brother Lawrence's *The Practice of the Presence of God*. As I read, I began to practice. I continually reminded myself that Jesus is with me, and every time I look to Him, His loving heart is touched… "One glance of your eye has ravished my heart…"

Brass Nugget 42: Joy Unexpected

Eight years had passed since I'd collected my first nugget. Though I had made much progress, my thought life could still bring me down.

In most books I had read, a profound experience changed a person forever. But that didn't happen for me. I seemed to have to learn the same lessons over and over again.

The worst of my weak points was guilt. Feelings of unworthiness often washed over me. At times I felt I was a terrible mother, that I had made a horrible mess of my life, that I was shallow and selfish and constantly let the Lord down. The enemy would remind me of every past failure over and over again.

Making the bed one morning early in that eighth year, these feelings of failure overwhelmed me, and I slumped onto the bed. After a moment, Jesus spoke into my heart, "What is the difference between accusation and conviction?"

Living in a household where legal discussions were regular dinner party conversation, the answer came quickly to mind. When an accusation is made, the accused must appear in court to defend himself. A conviction is made only after the court has tried the accused and found him guilty. In the spiritual realm, the Bible calls the enemy the accuser of the brethren. The devil can accuse, but he has no authority to convict. Only the Holy Spirit convicts.

The enemy brings the charge, the accusations, but it is God who passes judgment.

With my face in the pillow, it suddenly came to me as a breathtaking revelation that I desperately wanted to feel better about myself. Every time feelings of guilt and hopelessness washed over me, I tried to push the guilt away. But now, I looked at it full in the face. Yes. I was, indeed, guilty. The Holy God had tried me and found me guilty, and the conviction was read: "Condemned to hell for eternity."

I was struck by the full horror of what my future would be without Jesus. Oh, my Substitute, my Redeemer, my Saviour, my LORD!

Waves of love for Jesus washed over me, love as I had never known before. Deep, genuine love born of intense gratitude. It was the "Joy of my Salvation"! JOY! JOY! JOY! JOY!

I—the broken, weak, despairing one—had come to know the joy I longed for. It came, not from denying my sin, but from facing it, and finding afresh the wonder of Jesus' love.

Jesus said whoever has been forgiven much loves much, and now I understood how true that was. I loved Him with the passionate love of a prisoner released. The next time that familiar sense of guilt and failure swept over me, instead of pushing it away, I admitted my guilt. In stillness and silence, I imagined the agony of the Cross and realized afresh that my sin caused that agony. Not vague, collective sin, but my specific sin. Gratitude—humble gratitude—and an intense desire to love more and keep close to Jesus filled me every time I reviewed this reality.

The enemy still sent guilt to accuse me, but now, it didn't pull me into despair. Rather, it served as a potent reminder to look to Jesus.

Guilt is gone; now, with true conviction from the Holy Spirit comes the joy of being forgiven, accepted, and loved.

I don't remember where I read it, but someone said that the Christian life is begun with confession and is maintained by confession. Conviction, confession, and receiving forgiveness: these basics of the Christian life became for me a daily exercise to build tender love and sustaining strength.

The ballet parallel was obvious. True conviction of sin is simply the recognition of faults. The mirrors in a ballet studio are not there so the dancers can admire themselves, but so they can see their faults and work to correct them. God longs for the likeness of Jesus to be formed in us; for this to happen, we need to be corrected.

Ballet is exacting, the technique demanding. Tiny details the untrained eye would never detect are corrected over and over again. Even world-renowned professional dancers practice every day with a ballet master watching carefully for the tiniest thing that is not exactly correct.

No mature dancer would be offended by overzealous correction. In fact, they are disappointed if it is not given, for they know they cannot reach the highest possible standard without the eyes of the ballet master searching for the slightest flaw. But for the young dancer, constant encouragement must be given with gentle correction. Many a promising student has been broken by unrelenting, insensitive criticism. Good teachers train young dancers to recognize their own faults, to look for them in the mirror, and self-correct.

Jesus had carefully, lovingly, trained me, making me strong enough to cope with the shock of looking at myself in His mirror. To see how high is His standard, to see my faults, and to accept His correction. Eugene Peterson in *The Message* translates Matthew 11:28-30, "…Walk with me and work with me—watch how I do it. Learn the unforced rhythms of grace… ."

During those months of joyful confession, I re-read Roy Hession's *The Calvary Road*, where I found:

> As we walk with Him in the Light, He
> will be showing us all the time the
> beginnings of things which, if allowed to
> pass, will grieve Him and check the flow
> of His life in us…We must at no point
> protest our innocence of what He shows
> us… This demands that we must be men
> of a humble and contrite spirit, that is,
> men who are willing to be shown the
> smallest thing. But such are the ones,
> God says, who dwell with Him in the
> high and holy place.[31]

I told the Lord I was willing to be shown the smallest thing in my life that grieved Him. Over the following weeks and months, He showed me more and more faults. But I now knew the joy of release, the joy of loving One who loved me enough, through the pain and blood and jeers, to stay on that cross for me. I now knew beyond a doubt that He who died to bring me to Himself did not send suffering to punish, but to train. And it is truly a privilege to be under His schooling.

Brass Nugget 43: Joy Divine

Kaye had given me the *One Year Bible* for my birthday, with readings from the Old and New Testaments, Psalms, and Proverbs for each day. I never expected the book of Proverbs to reveal a life-changing nugget, and yet...

Proverbs 27:11 reads, "Be wise, my son, and bring joy to my heart; then I can answer anyone who treats me with contempt" (NIV).

Bring joy to my heart leapt from the page. Solomon is the speaker, I knew that. But as I read, those words seemed a tender command directly from the Lord. Jesus was asking me to be wise, to bring joy to His heart.

I had already learned I could bring Jesus joy simply by looking at Him, and also by quick confession. Now, this nugget revealed I could give Him joy by being wise. That much made sense, but what about the second part of the verse?

"Then I will be able to answer those who hold me in contempt."

Who holds God in contempt?

I used to avoid the book of Job, but over the past year, I had spent much time pondering it. The opening verses popped into my mind, and in an instant, I saw the enormity of all this little verse held.

God boasts about Job!

> Then the Lord said to Satan, "Have you
> considered my servant Job? There is no
> one on earth like him; he is blameless and
> upright, a man who fears God and shuns
> evil." (Job 1:8 NIV)

Satan's contemptuous reply insinuated that Job
only served God because He blessed him. I could
imagine Satan sniggering as he suggests that Job will
crack under suffering. It was now clear to me that it is
Satan who holds God in contempt.

Just imagine the joy God felt as Job proved Satan
wrong. Suffering did not crack Job. Suffering gave
Job the most precious gift: a deeper knowledge of
God: "My ears had heard of you but now my eyes
have seen you" (Job 42:5 NIV).

That very scenario was played out in my life
every day. Satan hoped if he just provoked me
enough, I would show God's trust in me was
unfounded.

I had been entrusted with suffering. I could
choose to allow it to teach me the deep lessons, or I
could descend into self-pity. Each time I chose to
lovingly "take up my cross," the Lord could know the
joy of boasting, "See, she is Mine!"

I longed to give my Lord this joy, yet I often
slipped back into the old ways.

Only a short time after discovering this nugget, I
read Psalm 38:16: "Do not let them gloat or exalt
themselves over me when my feet slip" (NIV).

When my feet slip, not *if*. The psalmist knew he would slip, and he prayed the evil one would not have reason to gloat. I realized that if I confessed my slips instantly and thanked Jesus that He had died to forgive me, the enemy could never gloat. Every time we praise Jesus for the cross, the enemy cringes and gnashes his teeth in anguish. Even my stumbling could be made to give glory to Jesus.

Some weeks after coming to this understanding, as I prayed, the Lord whispered, "Sit still and let me love you. Do not say anything. Just let Me love you. Allow yourself to receive My love. No, don't tell Me—I know you love me. Be still. Let Me love you."

So I sat still, very still.

Thoughts tried to interrupt, but my heart focused on Jesus' love. And it saturated my innermost being, wave after gentle wave, filling, soothing, healing. I realized I had never before been still enough to sense, or know, or allow the Lord to express His love to me.

At the end of the year of One Who Seeks His Face, I made a list of joy nuggets.

- I am loved with an everlasting love.
- Jesus is with me all the time.
- He is overcome by one glance of my eye.
- I bring Him joy every time I am wise and choose His way.
- It brings Jesus joy every time I confess.

These brass nuggets changed my life. They are simple yet powerful. Cramming my head full of scripture had not been able to help me escape the black well of depression because I knew scripture in the same way I knew my times tables; mere memorized facts held within my head, not living and breathing joy notes in my heart.

By knowing—really knowing, with every fibre of my being—that Jesus loves me, is with me always, and is longing for my looks of love, I have found rest.

Over time, this practice brought such delight that it has made me want to look toward Him more and more. But if I forgot, there was no guilt. I learned to relax into a loving relationship with my Lord, knowing that no matter what, He loves me still. He is watching me, loving me with the passion that took Him to the cross to save me. But when I look to Him, He smiles with pure joy; His loving heart is touched, and that thought makes me want to give him more glances of love.

My prayer life dramatically changed. Faith flowed in, bringing trust and assurance and rest. When I prayed for others, I did not need to plead with Jesus to be with them or to comfort them or strengthen them, as I *knew* He was with them, ready to give of Himself, offering to all His comfort, compassion, and love. I did not have to beg Him to do what He already offered. Instead, I prayed their spiritual eyes would be opened to receive all He longed to give them.

Jesus said He would never leave us, and He never has. Seeing Jesus as ever-present brought peace.

∽

Chapter 18

∽

Practicing, Not Pretending

YOU MAY ASK how all this practicing was any different from the acting and pretending I had been doing for so long. It is very different. Forcing myself to go through the motions drained me. Pretending was of no substance—it was a bright costume thrown over an empty wire mannequin, a hollow effort that could never be sustained.

There had been a black hole inside me that demanded to be filled, and I had tried to fill it by holding tightly to my rights, clutching thin cords of control, pulling in more and more—but the black hole could never be satisfied. Now, Jesus was in the centre of my being, and I rested in Him, relied on Him. Knowing He was there radiating light and life, I no longer had to pretend. I simply "worked out" what God had "worked in."

"Therefore... continue to work out your salvation with fear and trembling, for it is God who works in you to will and to act in order to fulfil His good purpose" (Philippians 2:12-13 NIV).

Paul sets forth the principle of God-powered practice: "To this end I strenuously contend with all the energy Christ so powerfully works in me" (Colossians 1:23 NIV).

I laboured, but it was God's power that gave me energy. I was working out my salvation, but it was God working in me. I no longer relied on my own effort to remain in control. I looked to my Teacher and followed His instructions—*and the dance flowed!*

The more I practiced, the more fluent and graceful the moves. It was often painful, and always costly to the self-life that cried out to be comforted. Self didn't like to be stretched; it was always trying to be heard, demanding its rights. But I would say, "I have no rights. I am a bond slave of Jesus. I want to serve Him, so I choose to be extended."

Practicing is hard at the beginning, but as with anything that is continually exercised, there comes a time when everything flows, gracefully, naturally, with no stress or striving. Another Fay Inchfawn quote became a favorite, "Let life flow warm from your hands."[32]

So I practiced letting the life of Jesus flow from my hands to all who came. The "difficult made to appear effortless" would take years of relentless practice.

Professional dancers can never take a holiday. Though they may not be performing, they must not stop stretching and practicing, or within a few weeks the body starts to return to its natural state. I understood what Oswald Chambers meant when he wrote, "You no more need a holiday from spiritual concentration than our heart needs a holiday from beating."[33]

∽

Chapter 19

∽

Full Circle

ONCE THE LORD has spoken a truth into the heart, He builds on that truth, revealing depths we can barely grasp, facets that delight, pathways that draw from us a longing to follow. Scripture builds on scripture. Study changes from dry duty to the unfolding of a love story.

And so it was with this next brass nugget. It was given to me years before I could see it at work in my life. I tried to include it earlier in this book, where it should have come in the timeline of my recovery, but somehow it didn't seem to fit. Only now do I see that this brass nugget is a summing-up that encapsulates all that I have learned.

Brass Nugget 44: Free Exchange

Going to the old chair in my ironing room, I found my Bible still open from the day before. As I leaned forward to pick it up, I read the words, "I will exchange your brass for gold" (Isaiah 60:17 TLB).

With tingling anticipation, I saw the link to the verse that had begun my journey. "…out of whose hills thou mayest dig brass" (Deuteronomy 8:9 KJV).

I saw the connection between the passages, but there was much more in this than I could grasp.

It was a random, insignificant verse, yet I felt a thrill.

"I will exchange your brass for gold."

Dropping to my chair, I prayed, *Lord, show me.*

I slowly came to see this was a promise of completion. Polishing brass nuggets requires effort, but gold shines without constant polishing. This was a promise that the things He had taught me would be established. The assurance swept me away: gold for brass. What a wonderful exchange!

I read on:

"I will exchange your iron for silver."

This also linked back to that first verse of the journey, Deuteronomy 8:9, "Whose stones are iron."

A doorway opened for me, an entry to a deep place. Though I could not grasp its full meaning, I knew it would lead to another level.

My stones had produced iron in me. I was stronger now. But what on earth did silver represent? This was something new. I spent days pondering it.

⁓

MY FRIENDS HAD just left after our weekly Bible study. I made several trips back and forth taking cups, saucers and crumb-covered cake plates from the sitting room to the kitchen. The last tray held my antique silver teapot, sugar bowl, and creamer. I set them down, then stood for a moment to appreciate their beauty. The phrase *silver service* popped into my mind.

Oh, I saw it! Iron is strong and practical, but silver is used for noble purposes.

I will exchange your iron for silver meant Jesus would exchange the strength extracted from my difficulties for beauty fit for His service. Oh, what a wonderful promise!

While washing the dishes, I thought of the silver coffeepot that lay in a dark corner of the pantry, badly tarnished. It was never used, as we had a modern coffee machine. Silver that is used regularly seldom needs harsh silver polish. A quick wash in hot soapy water and a vigorous buff with a dry tea towel is all that's required to keep it shining. What a vivid analogy! If the strengths I had gained were constantly used, they would always be shining, ready for His service. Suds flew from my rubber gloves as I threw my hands in the air in wonder.

The last two "exchanges" of Isaiah 60:17 were easier to understand.

"I will exchange your wood for brass."

In the Bible, wood is a symbol for sacrifice. It requires sacrifice to dig for brass in the midst of suffering. This verse was a confirmation of what had already taken place.

"I will exchange your stones for iron."

The whole journey had begun with this same promise in Deuteronomy 8:9. I was amazed how tenderly Jesus had brought me full circle.

A passage that seemed like nothing more than a list of unconnected objects was a logical progression! Those verses were like a conveyor belt. Hard lessons went on at one end, and I came out the other, totally changed.

It was a process:

> Stones are exchanged for iron, which is exchanged for silver = difficulties become strength, which leads to service.

> Wood is exchanged for brass, which is exchanged for gold = sacrifice becomes lessons, which when practiced produces godly character.

Stones ➡ Iron ➡ Silver

Difficulties ➡ Strength ➡ Service

Wood ➡ Brass ➡ Gold

Sacrifice ➡ Lessons ➡ Character

These verses are a joyful promise that God can transform the hard things of life into service for the King.

And the passage continues with wonderful promises:

> Peace and righteousness will be your
> taskmasters! (v. 17b) Violence will
> disappear out of your land—all war will
> end. Your walls will be "Salvation," and
> your gates "Praise". (Isaiah 60:17b-18,
> TLB)

Peace and righteousness will be your taskmasters.

A taskmaster was the slave master, the controller.
Until I accepted the circumstances of my life, they
controlled my actions and reactions—fear, anger,
retaliation, self-pity, and self-comfort. Now, as I look
to Jesus in the midst of my circumstances, the
focused desire for peace and righteousness dictates
my action. Therefore, peace and righteousness are
now my taskmasters.

*Violence will disappear out of your land. All war will
end.*

At the time this wonderful promise was given, I
was engaged in violent struggle against the
circumstances of my life and the symptoms of my
illness. Now, the promise is fulfilled, and its fulfilment
has come through the next part of the verse.

Your walls will be salvation.

Total trust in the finished work of Jesus is my
strong wall. I *know* Jesus loves me and is with me. He
who died to save me will never let anything come into
my life that cannot be used to draw me closer to Him.
Within that fortified tower, I am safe from the
tyranny of circumstances. Life here on earth will

always have problems, pain, and suffering, but now I trust that Jesus knows what He is doing.

I am not saying I don't pray for changes, because I most certainly do. God delights to answer prayer, and every day He is working miracles in the lives of countless millions. Over the years I have seen many answers to prayer: people delivered or healed in an instant—all amazing moves of the Sovereign God. I have had the privilege of seeing a mighty miracle in an intimate setting.

If, however, nothing changes after much prayer for healing, I do not go searching for reasons. I bow before the Father and pray with Jesus, "Your will be done."

I have heard it preached that to pray those words shows lack of faith. How could any prayer Jesus uttered be seen as lacking faith? And yet we were taught just that. "Name it, claim it, pray through to victory. Be specific, tell God what you want."

It sounds like the children of Israel demanding miracles in the desert, shouting defiantly, "Is God with us or not?" When we are in our personal desert, we want to shout at God and demand miracles. Yet acceptance brings softness and humility to the heart.

It took me years to come to the place of acceptance, but now, I am willing to allow whatever training method Jesus chooses for me.

And your gates praise.

The Lord has given me gates of praise. I praise Jesus for the stones He placed in my life. Not just lip service praise, but praise that comes from deeply considering the life-changing results of my difficulties. If I had received an instantaneous healing or if my life had been easier, I would never have grown into the person Jesus planned for me to be. I would have been a spoiled, pampered woman with no depth. These years of suffering have been a priceless gift, each stone a love token from my Jesus.

Deuteronomy 7:6 says, "Build an altar... with fieldstones" (NIV). I take that verse to mean that we are to gather the common, everyday difficulties and stand on top of them and shout praises to the Lord. It may be easy to praise the Lord for difficulties with the benefit of hindsight, but to praise Him while they are still sharp, troublesome, get-in-your-shoe-and-hurt-like-crazy stones? That is much harder. The altar of fieldstones is a thankful heart.

∞

Chapter 20

∞

Comfort

IF YOU'RE IN the midst of unbearable suffering, everything I have written screams insult to your pain. If you think, "Easy for her to talk; her problems were nothing compared to what I am going through," you are right. What I have written is totally inadequate to meet your need.

But there is One who knows your whole story, and I trust Him to speak between these lines and bring comfort to your breaking heart.

I know the questions that rise up to taunt you, the anger and the torment, the frantic prayers, the desperation. I used to badger Jesus for miracles. Prosperity teaching urged me to "pray through to victory," to keep pounding away. I prayed until I was utterly worn out by the constant striving.

I felt like that poor little woman in Luke 18:1-5, pleading her case before the unjust judge. She never let up until she wore him down, and he gave her what she wanted just to keep her quiet. That parable used to made me feel uneasy. I could not understand Jesus' example of the unjust judge.

Pondering this one morning, I realized I had been seeing God as unjust; my emotions told me God was not fair to have allowed my suffering. And then it was as if in my heart I heard Jesus whisper, "Still you have followed Me all this way. You never let Me go."

That day, I came to believe the lesson of the parable is not to keep badgering, but to keep following. Even if our emotions scream, "God is unjust," follow Him still. Cling to Him. Abandon all to Him.

Suffering is a profound darkness. We stumble along, blind with grief, and cannot see a way ahead. In our private darkness we feel that the Lord has forsaken us, but He has not; He is tenderly close, gently guiding.

This promise was precious to me in my dark days:

> I will lead the blind by ways they have not known, along unfamiliar paths I will guide them; I will turn the darkness into light before them and make the rough places smooth. These are the things I will do; I will not forsake them." (Isaiah 24:16, NIV)

You are not alone in the dark. He is with you, suffering with you, feeling your pain. Trust Him; He has a purpose. The darkness is a rite of passage.

In Hannah Hurnard's *Hinds Feet on High Places*, the Shepherd says to Much-Afraid as he leads her through a burning desert:

> All of my servants on their way to the High Places have to make this detour through the desert. It is called "The furnace of Egypt, and a horror of great darkness." Here they have learned many things which otherwise they would have known nothing about...It is a great privilege, and if you will, you also may learn the lesson of the furnace and of the great darkness just as surely as did those before you. Those who come down to the furnace go on their way afterwards as royal men and women, princes and princesses of the Royal Line.[34]

And so it will be with you. Through suffering, you enter into fellowship with Jesus along a path that is mysterious, deep, and true. Though there may be months or even years of groping to find your way, there will come a time when you will know the wonder of His touch and hear His whisper. When your time of darkness is over, you will have words of comfort to share with others: "What I tell you in the dark, speak in the daylight" (Matthew 10:27, NIV). From the darkness of your suffering can come a shining brilliance that will illuminate your life and the lives of others.

I want to shout, "Suffering is not a sign of spiritual failure!" It is a sign of being chosen for special training.

"I have chosen thee in the furnace of affliction" (Isaiah 48:1b KJV).

Charles Spurgeon writes of the verse above:

> This has long been the motto fixed before our eye upon the wall of our bedroom, and in many ways it has also been written on our hearts… We are chosen as an afflicted people and not as a prosperous people, chosen not in the palace but in the furnace. In the furnace beauty is marred, fashion is destroyed, strength is melted, glory is consumed, and yet here eternal love reveals its secrets and declares its choice. So has it been in our case. In time of severest trial God has made to us our calling and election plain, and we have made it sure: then have we chosen the Lord to be our God, and He has shown that we are assuredly His chosen. Therefore, if today the furnace be heated seven times hotter, we will not dread it, for the glorious Son of God will walk with us amid the glowing coals.[35]

Jesus knows what it is to suffer. Jesus taught us to pray, "Your will be done," and then He lived those words in Gethsemane.

Jesus accepted the cup of suffering from His Father's hand.

Do not see your suffering as from the hand of the enemy. Satan is not all-knowing and cannot anticipate the plans of God. If he could, he never would have incited evil men to crucify Jesus. At the cross, Satan was arrogant enough to think he had out-maneuvered God. Yet he unwittingly carried out God's own plan of making salvation freely available. Satan could not see that by his actions, he was about to set in motion his own downfall: "And having disarmed the powers and authorities, He made a public spectacle of them, triumphing over them by the cross" (Colossians 2:5 NIV).

Suffering has many biblical metaphors: darkness, valleys, slippery pits, storms, mountains, stones, and deserts. No matter what you call it, suffering is lonely. No one else can walk with us. No friend, no family member—though they may try, they are unable to enter in. But there is One who is with us all the time. He longs to feel the first tentative pressure of our hand as we reach to Him. In fact, He longs for more than that small touch. He longs for us to lean on Him, to put upon Him our full weight.

"Who is this that comes up out of the desert leaning on her Beloved?" (Song of Solomon 8:5 NIV).

There is intimacy in the desert; it is there we learn to call Him Beloved.

∞

Chapter 21

∞

A Journey of Your Own

I HAVE TAKEN you, in the space of a few chapters, on a journey that took me over nine years to make. As I read through my manuscript, I feel I have made the journey seem far more seamless than it was. Stumbling, falling, failing, I struggled through these years. There are many more little nuggets and steps that I have not included, all of them precious to me.

I never understood Matthew 13:12, "Whoever has will be given more, and they will have an abundance. Whoever does not have, even what they have will be taken from them" (NIV).

It took me years to learn Jesus was speaking of spiritual treasure. These little brass nuggets are my treasure. Each time I carefully stored a nugget in my heart, treasuring it and polishing it, Jesus would give me another, and when that nugget was polished, still another, slowly building up a rich store. I noticed He never gave me a new brass nugget until I had acted upon the preceding one, even in the smallest way.

Jesus said, "He who has much will be given more." To *have* a thing is to own it, to make it yours. As I polished my brass, it became truly mine. I owned it in my heart, and so was given more. When I had little, the enemy was able to rob me until I became so impoverished I slid into depression, the well of black waters on "Hill Difficulty."

Andrew Murray writes:

> But we know that all God bestows needs
> time to become fully our own; it must be
> held fast and appropriated and
> assimilated into our inmost being.
> Without this, not even Christ's giving can
> make it our very own in full experience
> and enjoyment.[36]

This book of my journey began with one brass nugget scribbled in a notebook. Jesus longs to take you on your own journey. One that will be exciting and revealing and uniquely yours. It all begins with one nugget.

Please, please, do not take what I have written as a formula to follow. Remember, I am no one special. Every day I must choose to deny myself, take up my cross, and follow Him. Seek to know Jesus in a deeper way, forget about formulas, and draw close to Him, for each one is special to Him, and He deals with each of us in a unique way. Ask Jesus to reveal to you afresh some forgotten nugget, something He spoke into your heart long ago, brass that He wants you to have as gold.

I recommend that you journal your experiences. Record these treasures where they will not be lost, and review them often. Include them in your prayers, think about them through the day; polish each until it shines like gold, and then add the next pieces of brass as the Lord gives them to you.

Guard your treasure carefully, for the enemy is always waiting to rob, steal, and destroy. Catch those subtle thoughts that lead the heart away, and quickly bring your eyes back to Jesus. Your treasury will grow; Jesus will add to it as you continue to polish what you have.

Brass nuggets can come from many unexpected sources: a familiar verse seen in a new light, the words of a song, a line from a book, a chance comment from a stranger, or from the loving words of a friend. So be on the lookout for them. One nugget can begin a gold rush; they are "treasures out of darkness," and they will lead you to an adventure with your Beloved that will continually change your life until your eyes meet His at the wedding feast.

> So you will ride at ease over the breakers of this mortal life and not care too much what befalls you, not for carelessness, but from the soaring gladness of heavenly love.[37]

∞

Footnote

∞

I WANT TO make it very clear that I am not suggesting "accepting our stones" means it is the will of God for women to stay in abusive relationships. That is definitely not the case!

Ecclesiastes 3:5 (KJV) says, "There is a time to cast away stones and a time to gather stones together."

The stones God sends into our lives can be used constructively, but an abusive relationship is destructive and should be cast away. Staying in such a relationship is what psychologists call co-dependency, and co-dependency is not a healthy, normal way of thinking.

A number of Christian psychologists suggest that some churches foster the mental disorder of co-dependency either actively (by encouraging women to stay in destructive marriages) or passively (by not offering them the support they need to leave). Unaided, a person trapped in a co-dependent relationship lacks the strength to break free from the bonds of wrong thinking built up over a lifetime.

I cannot stress strongly enough that if you are in a marriage where there is violence, drug or alcohol abuse, repeated infidelity, or any other form of abuse, including manipulative and controlling behaviour, trust Jesus to help you break free. Do not think by staying you will be able to save your spouse. Christian psychologists call that way of thinking the "Messiah Syndrome." When I first read that term it shocked me, as I felt that it was almost blasphemy. But it is a true description of the thinking of a Christian who stays in an abusive marriage to "save my spouse."

You cannot save an abusive spouse. Only Jesus can save. By staying, you are not doing God's work but are hindering it; for by staying, you condone the wrong behaviour and so unwittingly prevent your spouse from suffering the consequences of his actions.

For the abusive spouse, true repentance is necessary. Often, abusers who attend church will play the repentance card over and over again, pretending remorse in order to maintain control over their victim. Many will throw the forgiveness card: "You must forgive me. You are a Christian." They may even quote Jesus' command to forgive someone "seventy time seven" (Matthew 18:21-22). If you are caught up in a destructive relationship, remember that Jesus loves you, and it is not His will for you to be abused!

You can continue to pray for your spouse from a safe place, but don't be tempted to play the "leaving-then-running-back-only-to-leave-again" game. Those are the actions of a truly co-dependent person. If this is the pattern that you have established in your life, seek the help of a qualified counsellor. I highly recommend the Christian psychology book *Love is a Choice: Breaking the Cycle of Addictive Relationships* by Robert Hemfelt, Frank Minirth, and Paul Meier.

Do not listen to those who tell you that you should just hang in there and pray. There is a time for prayer, and God does work miracles; but He can work the miracles without you being in the war zone.

Co-dependents believe there can be no happiness for them unless they are with their spouse no matter how destructive the relationship may be. They have come to wrongly believe their love is overwhelming and uncontrollable, that only this love and no other will satisfy. In short, it is an addiction. If you are caught in this trap, give it all over to Jesus: the mind games, the "if I do this then my spouse will do that" mentality. Instead, throw yourself upon Jesus and make *Him* the focus of your love. You will find that He will so fill you and strengthen you that you will be able to live in a normal way without the crippling addiction to your destructive spouse.

If you are in a church where you constantly feel condemned, I highly recommend the classic *The Subtle Power of Spiritual Abuse* by David Johnson and Jeff Van Vonderen. It is readable, moving, and helpful. Its dedication reads: "To the weary and heavy laden, deeply loved by God, but because of spiritual abuse, find that the Good News has somehow become the bad news."

The lie that prayers remain unanswered because some key or formula is missing caused me years of anguish. Prayer is not dependent on our puny words! It is the awesome power of the cross, the obedience of Jesus, that is the evil one's undoing. I firmly believe that when we turn the eyes of our spirit upon our lovely Jesus, even wordlessly, demons run. Jesus has won the victory. Hallelujah!

An old hymn says, "Satan trembles when he sees the weakest Christian on their knees."

Far too much has been written about spiritual warfare. We can have our heads stuffed full with this teaching. All we need to know is that Jesus loves us and He never leaves us!

Eugene Patterson in *The Message* translates Matthew 6:7-8:

"The world is full of so-called prayer warriors who are prayer-ignorant They're full of formulas and programs and advice, peddling techniques for getting what you want from God. Don't fall for that nonsense. This is your Father you are dealing with and he knows better than you what you need. With a God like this loving you, you can pray very simply."

For a more in-depth look at the errors of Prosperity Teaching, Word of Faith, etc., see:

- *Christianity in Crisis* by Hank Hanegraaff
- *Too Good to be True: Finding Hope in a World of Hype* by Michael Horton
- *A Different Gospel* by Dan McConnell

∽

Additional Note

∽

Kaye and friends continue to meet together, laughing and sharing the classics of Christian literature. They encouraged me to write this book, and all send their love.

Edith Harrington

∽

Endnotes

∽

[1] Rebecca Lee Wai Yue, *I Have Loved You. The Resource Chorus Book*, Praise and Worship Words Book No. 1, Resource Christian Music (Mary Borough, Victoria: Australian Print Group, 1981).

[2] From *Prayers Written at Vailima*, Robert Louis Stevenson, 1890, quoted by Mrs. Charles E. Cowman, *Springs in the Valley*, (Los Angeles, CA: Cowman Publications, Inc., 1950), 202.

[3] Cowman, *Springs in the Valley*, 107.

[4] H. V. Morton, *In the Steps of St. Paul* (London: Rich & Cowan LTD, 1936), 37.

[5] Mrs. Charles E. Cowman, *Travelling Toward Sunrise* (Los Angeles, CA: Cowman Publications, Inc, 1952), 174.

[6] Peter J. Madden, *The Wigglesworth Standard* (Kensington, PA: Whitaker House, 1993), back cover.

[7] Ibid, 148.

[8] Ibid.

[9] Ibid, p. 146.

[10] Ibid.

[11] Ibid.

[12] Isobel Kuhn, *Green Leaf in Drought* (Great Britain: Overseas Missionary Fellowship, 1978), 57.

[13] *His Thoughts Said . . . His Father Said . . .* by Amy Carmichael, ©1941 by The Dohnavur Fellowship. Used by permission of CLC Publications. May not be further reproduced. All rights reserved.

[14] Ibid, 69.

[15] A. W. Tozer, *The Pursuit of God* (Camp Hill, PA: Christian Publications, Inc, 1997), 26.

[16] Mrs. Charles E. Cowman, *Streams in the Desert* (Los Angeles, CA: Cowman Publications, Inc., 1970), 23.

[17] This material is taken from *My Utmost for His Highest* by Oswald Chambers, edited by James Reimann, copyright © 1992 by Oswald Chambers Publications Assn., Ltd. Original edition copyright © 1935 by Dodd Mead & Co., renewed 1963 by the Oswald

Chambers Publications Assn., Ltd. Used by permission of Discovery House Publishers, Box 3566, Grand Rapids MI 49501. All rights reserved.

[18] Ibid, 312.

[19] Ibid, 255.

[20] Ibid, 321.

[21] D. J. Butler, *I Will Change Your Name* (Mercy/Vineyard Publishing 1987).

[22] "In Acceptance Lieth Peace," Mountain Breezes: The Collected Poems of Amy Carmichael by Amy Carmichael, 1999 by The Dohnavur Fellowship. Used by permission of CLC Publications. May not be further reproduced. All rights reserved.

[23] Rita Snowden, *If I Open My Door* (London: Epworth Press, 1937), 214-215

[24] *Rose from Brier* by Amy Carmichael, ©1933 by The Dohnavur Fellowship. Used by permission of CLC Publications. May not be further reproduced. All rights reserved.

[25] Cowman, *Springs in the Valley*, p. 57.

[26] Chambers, *My Utmost*, 195.

[27] Andrew Murray, *Abide in Christ* (Kensington, PA: Whitaker House, 1979), 31.

[28] William C. Gannett, *Blessed Be Drudgery* (Glasgow: David Bryce and Son, 1890, Preface by the Countess of Aberdeen.

[29] Chambers, *My Utmost For His Highest*, 44.

[30] Tozer, *The Pursuit of God*, 55.

[31] Roy Hession, *Calvary Road* (London: Christian Literature Crusade, 1950), 107.

[32] Fay Inchfawn was the pen name of Elizabeth Rebecca Ward, a prolific English writer of verse, religious books, and children's stories during the years between the two World Wars. I have read a number of her works, but I have not been able to locate the one this quote comes from.

[33] Chambers, *My Utmost*, 112.

[34] Some content taken from HIND'S FEET ON HIGH PLACES by Hannah Hurnard. Copyright *1975. Used by permission of Tyndale House Publishers, Inc. All rights reserved.

[35] Charles H. Spurgeon, *Faith's Checkbook: 365-Day Devotional* (Kensington, PA: Whitaker House, 1992), 246.

[36] Murray, *Abide in Christ*, 20.

[37] Maud Monahan, *Life and Letters of Janet Erskine Stuart* (New York: Longmans, Green & Co., 1937), 1.

Bibliography

Bunyan, John. *Pilgrim's Progress.* Public domain.

Carmichael, Amy. *His Thoughts Said … His Father Said….* India: Dohnavur Fellowship, 1941.

Carmichael, Amy. *Mountain Breezes: The Collected Poems of Amy Carmichael.* India: Dohnavur Fellowship, 1999.

Carmichael, Amy. *Rose From Brier.* India: Dohnavur Fellowship, 1957.

Chambers, Oswald. *My Utmost For His Highest.* UK: Oswald Chambers Publications Association, 1927.

Cowman, Mrs. Chas. E. *Springs in the Valley.* Los Angeles, CA: Cowman Publications, Inc., 1950.

Cowman, Mrs Chas. E. *Travelling Toward Sunrise.* Los Angeles, CA: Cowman Publications, Inc, 1952.

Cowman, Mrs. Chas. E. *Streams in the Desert.* Los Angeles, CA: Cowman Publications, Inc., 1925 (reprinted 1970).

Foxe, John. *Foxe's Book of Martyrs.* First published in England by John Day in 1563 with the original title of *Actes and Monuments of these Latter and Perillous Days, Touching Matters of the Church.* The edition referred to in the text was published by Bridge Logos, Inc. in Orlando, FL.

Gannett, William C. *Blessed Be Drudgery.* Glasgow: David Bryce and Son, 1890.

Hanegraaff, Hank. *Christianity in Crisis.* Nashville, TN: Thomas Nelson, Inc., 2009.

Hemfelt, Robert, Minirth, Frank, Meier, Paul. *Love is a Choice.* Nashville, TN: Thomas Nelson, Inc. 1989.

Herman, Nicholas (calling himself Brother Lawrence). *The Practice of the Presence of God*. Revised and rewritten by Chadwick, Harold S. North Brunswick, NJ: Bridge-Logos Publishers, 1999.Horton, Michael. *Too Good to be True....* Grand Rapids, MI: Zondervan, 2006.

Hurnard, Hannah. *Hinds' Feet on High Places*. Wheaton, IL: Tyndale House Publisher, Inc., 1975.

Johnson, David, Vonderen, Jeff. *The Subtle Power of Spiritual Abuse*. Minneapolis, MN: Bethany House Publishers, 1991.

Kuhn, Isobel. *Green Leaf in Drought*. Great Britain: Overseas Missionary Fellowship, 1978.

Madden, Peter J. *The Wigglesworth Standard*. New Kensington, PA: Whitaker House, 1993.

McConnell, Dan R. *A Different Gospel*. Peabody, MA: Hendrickson Publishers, 2011.

Monahan, Maud. *Life and Letters of Janet Erskine Stuart*. New York: Longmans, Green & Co., 1937.

Morton, H.V. *In the Steps of St. Paul*. London, UK: Rich & Cowan LTD, 1936.

Murray, Andrew. *Abide in Christ*. Kensington, PA: Whitaker House, 1979.

Sinker, George. *Jesus Loved Martha: The Housewife's Contacts With Jesus*. London: St. Hugh's Press, 1949.

Snowden, Rita F. *If I Open My Door*. London: Epworth Press, 1937.

Spurgeon, Charles H. *Faith's Checkbook: 365-Day Devotional*. Kensington, PA: Whitaker House, 1992.

Tozer, A. W. *The Pursuit of God*. Camp Hill, PA: Christian Publications, Inc., 1997.

Yue, Rebecca Lee Wai. *The Resource Chorus Book*, *Praise and Worship Words Book No. 1*, Resource Christian Music. Mary Borough, Victoria: Australian Print Group, 1981.

I would not lose the hard things from my life,
The rocks o'er which I stumbled long ago,
The griefs and fears, the failures and mistakes,
That tried and tested faith and patience so,
I need them now: they make the deep-laid wall,
The firm foundation-stones on which I raise-
To mount therein from stair to higher stair
The lofty towers of my House of Praise.

(author unknown)

CPSIA information can be obtained
at www.ICGtesting.com
Printed in the USA
FFHW022329091218
49769742-54250FF

9 781946 985057